ART IN THE AGE OF IMPERIALISM AND SOCIALISM

PETER HACKS

Art in the Age of Imperialism and Socialism

Essays, Poems, Prose, and a Playlet

EDITED BY SHASWATI MAZUMDAR AND KAI KÖHLER

LEFTWORD

First published in April 2025

LeftWord Books
2254/2A Shadi Khampur
New Ranjit Nagar
New Delhi 110008
INDIA

LeftWord Books and Vaam Prakashan are imprints of
Naya Rasta Publishers Pvt. Ltd.

leftword.com

ISBN 978-93-92018-95-4 (paperback)
978-93-92018-56-5 (e-book)

Contents

Abbreviations 9

Peter Hacks – Iconoclast and Classicist: Introduction 11

(AUTO-)BIOGRAPHICAL

Personal Particulars 31
Anecdotes by Hacks 33
Anecdotes by André Müller in Collaboration with Hacks 40

POLITICAL

Letter to the German-African Society 49
On the War of Aggression in Vietnam 50
"A Revolution Against the State?" Questions in the Title and Seven Others 53
How Are Things in Socialism's Public Offices? 59
The Latest from Biermann 63
The Little Men With Their Ballheads 68
Letter to a Lady in Paris About a Place Called Germany 70
The Worst Socialism is Still Better Than the Best Capitalism 72
The Task Before Us The Restoration of a Revolution Cut Short 74
The Names of the Left 77
Georg Nostradamus or the Predictions of Professor Fülberth 81
Dispute at the Wailing Wall 94
In the End They Even Understand It 95

ON ART AND AESTHETICS

Literature in the Age of Science	101
Brecht's Aesthetics	103
Answers to 4 questions	104
From the Foreword to the Essay "The Poetic"	108
The Entrance March of Demetrius Or: Theatre as Pomp	111
Art and Revolution	116
Butzbach Author Survey	118
Saving Christianity from the Christians	119
Note on Young Writers in the GDR	121
Information for America	122
[Ideal and Utopia]	125
Foreword to the Essay "Determinations"	126
From the Essay "Poetic Commerce"	129
Under the Media, the Muses Fall Silent Foundations of a Science	141
[Left-Wing Art]	164

STORIES AND POEMS

[Two Heavenly Tales]	167
Ameli and the Frog Prince	168
The Man from Sing-Sing	170
The Wench Factory of Tahoua	172
The Royal Court Moves House	175
Frau Thousand-feet Must Wash Today	178
Errors	179
Ladislaus and Komkarlinchen	180
News of the Life of the Perамblers	182
October Song	184
Strike Song	186
Lumumba's Death	188
You Shall Deny Me Nothing	190
1. 8. 1973	191

Ask Not Whether Love is Worth It 192
Asides 193
Trying Times 194
The Little Unicorns 195
Make Haste, O You Hours 196
Couplets 197
The Thirty Tyrants 201
My Precious Nation 203
1990 206
Fragile Multi-People State 207
Venus and Stalin 209
Monument to a Monument (2) 210
The Party 211
Now-time 212

A PLAYLET
The Bishop of China 217

FOR THE RECORD
Autobiography [1965] 239

Persons Index 241
Translators and Sources 249

Abbreviations

APO Extra-parliamentary opposition; left-wing political protest movement in West Germany mainly during the 1960s; closely allied with the 1968 student movement.

CIA Central Intelligence Agency; US foreign intelligence agency engaged in espionage and covert political and paramilitary operations across the world.

CPSU Communist Party of the Soviet Union

DFU German Peace Union, small left-wing party that existed in West Germany from 1960 to 1984.

DKP German Communist Party, oriented to the Soviet Union; refoundation in 1968 in West Germany of the KPD, which had been banned in 1956.

FDP Free Democratic Party; oriented to economic liberalism, founded in 1948 in West Germany.

FRG Federal Republic of Germany

GDR German Democratic Republic

KAPD Communist Workers' Party of Germany; founded in 1920 after the split with the KPD, oriented to council-communism.

KGB Committee for State Security; Soviet security and intelligence agency from 1954 until the collapse of the Soviet Union in 1991.

KPD Communist Party of Germany, founded in 1918, banned from 1933 to 1945. It merged in the Soviet occupied zone in 1946 with the SPD to form the SED. In the FRG, it was banned again in 1956. Refounded in 1990 by SED members who opposed the reformist transformation into the PDS.

KPD/ML Communist party founded in West Germany in 1968; initially oriented to Maoism, and then to Enver Hoxha of the Communist Party of Albania.

NPD National Democratic Party of Germany; neo-Nazi party founded in 1964.

PDS Party of Democratic Socialism in Germany; left social democratic refoundation of the SED in 1990.

PEN International association of writers aimed at promoting peace, freedom of expression and cooperation across borders.

PCI Communist Party of Italy; founded in 1921 after the split from the PSI; after World War II it became the second largest party in Italy and the largest communist party in the West.

PSI Italian Socialist Party, socialist and later social-democratic party in Italy; founded in 1892, dominated the Italian left till the end of World War II.

RAF Red Army Faction, also known as the Baader–Meinhof Group; leftwing urban guerrilla group in West Germany engaged during the 1970s and 1980s in armed resistance against the state.

SAP	Socialist Workers' Party of Germany; left-wing socialist party that split from the SPD in 1931.
SED	Socialist Unity Party of Germany; created in 1946 through the merger of the KPD and SPD, it became the ruling party in the GDR. Refoundation as PDS in 1990.
SPD	Social Democratic Party of Germany
USA/US	United States of America
USPD	Independent Social Democratic Party of Germany, founded in 1917 as a left-wing split from the SPD in protest against the latter's support for the war.
USSR	Union of Soviet Socialist Republics or the Soviet Union.

Peter Hacks – Iconoclast and Classicist: Introduction

> Admittedly, art is a weapon. Admittedly, a mallet is a weapon. According to Aristotle, it does not follow that art must be a mallet.
> Rather, it follows that art is all the better a weapon, the more artistic it is.
>
> (Peter Hacks: 'Art and Revolution')

LIFE AND TIMES

Who was Peter Hacks? A German playwright who wrote poetry, essays, and prose, including several works for children. Hacks is recognised as one of the most important writers of the German Democratic Republic. A writer who, as a young man shortly after the Second World War, chose to migrate from West to East Germany – i.e., from a capitalist to a socialist society – and held to this choice even after the GDR was incorporated into the Federal Republic of Germany and ceased to exist. The title of this anthology points to the major factors that define his work, aesthetically and politically. In both aesthetics and politics, he stood apart from the general tendencies of his time, achieving renown and a good many prizes with (and sometimes despite) his sharp-tongued, witty and utterly delightful writing. In fact, he was, at times, one of the most performed playwrights, not only in the GDR but also in the FRG.

In the times we live in, it is the singular nature of this writer and his work, the fact that he is aesthetically unfashionable and politically unpalatable, that have caused him to be hidden from public view. Since this is largely the case in the universe of German speakers, it is not surprising that he is practically unknown in the English-speaking world. This, the editors believe, is a loss that needs to be rectified. This volume is an effort in that direction.

Peter Hacks lived through tumultuous times. He was born in 1928 in the backdrop of the rise of fascism. He witnessed its rule and defeat, the Second World War and its aftermath, the division of Germany and Europe into the capitalist West and the socialist East, the difficulties of implementing socialism while facing powerful hostile forces abroad and the eventual collapse of socialism in the GDR and Eastern Europe. Until his death in 2003, he remained recalcitrant and irreverent in his political views and disdainful of what he considered newfangled notions in aesthetics.

Born to parents who were socialists and antifascists, Hacks tried unsuccessfully to evade military service in the final days of the Second World War, was taken prisoner by the Nazis, forcefully drafted into the official paramilitary labour service and subsequently held as a prisoner of war by the Americans. After the war, he went to university in Munich, where he also started to emerge as a writer, initially for radio and cabaret, before he earned recognition as a playwright in 1954 with his play 'Eröffnung des indischen Zeitalters' (Opening of the Indian Era), for which he won the Prize for Young Writers of the City of Munich. The play stages the voyages of Columbus to the Americas; the opening of the Indian era is the era of capitalism – an era characterised simultaneously by the colossal improvement of human potential and the colossal horrors of colonial expropriation. The play's focus is on the relationship, within this context, of the imaginable to the achievable, a central feature of Hacks' plays.

MIGRATION TO EAST GERMANY

In 1955, soon after the staging of his Columbus play and his emergence in the many reviews as a rising dramatic talent, Hacks migrated to East Berlin, the capital of the GDR, after corresponding with Bertolt Brecht about his wish to make this move.[1] Brecht

1 The Cold War had already begun almost immediately after the allies of the Second World War (the Soviet Union, the US, Britain, and France) celebrated victory over fascism. NATO (military alliance of the US, Canada and

had returned from exile after the defeat of fascism and settled in the GDR, where he could establish his own theatre, the Berliner Ensemble. In his initial reply to Hacks, Brecht had said, "Good people are good everywhere". However, Hacks remained adamant since he found the capitalist West no longer stimulating for his writing. After settling in East Berlin, he worked with Brecht at the Berliner Ensemble for a while and became, along with the playwright Heiner Müller, one of the most prominent representatives of the Brecht school. After Brecht's death in 1956, he moved to the Deutsches Theater, another prominent theatre in East Berlin. He began developing his own conception of theatre and aesthetics in a direction away from Brecht's influence. Whereas Brecht had been more concerned with the *antagonistic* contradictions of capitalist society, Hacks and many of his contemporaries in the GDR were inevitably more interested in the *non-antagonistic* contradictions emerging in the process of building socialism.

While Hacks had so far set his plays in the past, though always as a reflection of the present, he now looked for dramatic material in the socialist present. The play 'Die Sorgen und die Macht' (Worries and the State), conceptualised as a post-revolutionary drama, is set among factory workers caught up in the friction between the urgent need for quantity in output versus the equally compelling need for quality in a planned economy. Individual versus collective aspirations played out within this context. Performed against the backdrop of an escalating Cold War and the construction of the Berlin Wall to halt the drain of skilled professionals, the play was misunderstood and banned by the government after 22 successful performances. This was also the period in which Hacks experimented with agitprop writing, including short plays and poems set to music and broadcast on radio. Two examples included in this volume are 'October Song' and 'Strike Song'.

the capitalist states in Western Europe) was established in April 1949. In response, the Warsaw Pact (military alliance of the Soviet Union and the socialist states in Eastern Europe) was signed in May 1955.

At around the same time, Hacks won acclaim with the hugely successful staging of his adaptation of Aristophanes' Greek comedy 'Der Frieden' (Peace). The focus of the adaptation was not primarily on criticism of war but rather on the struggle against those who profit from it, a struggle aimed at enjoying the fruits of peace: happiness based on the satisfaction of people's material needs. With its witty language and trenchant humour, the play also highlighted Hacks' predisposition to comedy and the comic in general. The tumultuous applause at the premiere went on for forty-five minutes. Its success marked the beginning of Hacks' rise as one of the GDR's leading playwrights, celebrated both for the quality of his works and their popularity with audiences. And although his support for the building of the Berlin Wall made him a target of criticism and calls for boycott in West Germany, he was among the first GDR playwrights to enjoy a big breakthrough with theatre audiences in both German states. His monodrama 'Ein Gespräch im Hause Stein über den abwesenden Herrn von Goethe' (A conversation in the Stein house about the absent Herr von Goethe, 1974) became an international success. It was staged at more than 200 theatres in both German states and in 25 other countries. The play is a monologue by the noblewoman Charlotte von Stein about the poet Goethe. The social backdrop is the dukedom of Weimar, where the much-feted poet had been made a minister. The lady complains about the poet's rude behaviour towards other members of the court and castigates his political views (in favour of abolishing the tax exemption for the nobility). But her tirades mask her love for him. Hacks found the tensions of this setting still relevant: Socialism had yet to find a befitting place for two kinds of people, namely for women and for geniuses.

The adaptation of Aristophanes' play also marks Hacks' turn away from the present to classical antiquity, mythology and historical settings for his dramas. This was not motivated by the political troubles he had faced with contemporary settings but rather by the perception that dramas set in the present were less amenable to poetic treatment. This is why, he argued, the Greek tragedians, Shakespeare and the poets of German classicism did not write such plays.

Hacks' views on art and politics were often not in line with official policy and he was embroiled in several controversies. Yet he remained consistent in his commitment to socialism and the GDR. In the political controversies during his life, he insisted on taking a class position against morally defined ones. During the period when he enjoyed popularity in the theatres in the West, Western critics attempted to cast him as a dissident, but they were mistaken. Matters came to a head with the so-called Biermann affair in 1976 when the dissident poet and songwriter Wolf Biermann was stripped of his GDR citizenship while visiting West Germany for a performance in Cologne. Several of the most well-known GDR writers signed a protest petition, but Hacks refused to join them, instead expressing support for the government's action. Following this, Hacks was sharply attacked by critics in the East and the West. His unsparing, sardonic criticism of Biermann and what he represented can be found in the essay in this volume, 'The Latest from Biermann'.

COLLAPSE OF SOCIALISM AND AFTERMATH

Beginning with the seventies, Hacks observed, with growing disquiet and foreboding, what he saw as revisionist tendencies in socialism and a process of conciliation with imperialism. His perceptions and criticism also found their way into his plays. Nevertheless, he was not prepared for the ultimate collapse of the GDR and its incorporation into the FRG. Convinced that he would live out his life under socialism, to which he had dedicated his artistic endeavours, he suddenly found himself like a fish out of water. Undoubtedly embittered by this unanticipated turn of events, Hacks responded with defiance and disdain towards those who sought to reconcile and accommodate themselves to the new political environment. On Brecht's birth centenary in 1998, the left-wing newspaper *Neues Deutschland* asked various writers to name their favourite Brecht poem. Hacks decided to choose the 'Song of the class enemy' with its emphatic lines: "And whatever I still may learn / This is the bottom-line: / Won't ever join the class enemy / It's cause can never be mine."

In the one and a half decades from the end of the GDR till his death, Hacks returned with a vengeance to his writing, though he was now impelled by the *antagonistic* contradictions of capitalist society, which he had thought to have escaped when he migrated to the GDR. He also wrote a number of essays on art and politics, the publication of which once again drew the attention of critics to his provocative but incisive and elegant style. As these critics point out, even those distant from Hacks' political ideas have to acknowledge his literary abilities.

Several epithets have been used to describe this writer with his unrepentant views and scathing criticism of those he held responsible for the downfall of socialism: an oddball or even an enfant terrible of GDR literature, politically eccentric but a captivating writer, an aristocratic Marxist, an anti-dogmatic dogmatist and a classical writer. His views on art were sometimes construed as an escape from politics into history or mythology, at other times as aesthetically regressive; some critics also tried to separate his art from his politics. In fact, they were innately linked and precisely thought out. His goal was no less than to lay the groundwork for a socialist literature.

ART FOR A SOCIALIST SOCIETY

Before moving to the GDR, Hacks was, of course, opposed to the political environment around him: to the Nazi regime in any case, but also to the West German restoration of capitalism in the 1950s. Criticism of authorities or even religion was not welcome, especially in the very Christian Bavaria where he grew up. The irreverent tone of his earliest works, inspired by the 19th century German poet Heinrich Heine, not to mention his links to cabaret, did not correspond to the ideal of the dignified poet of society. Hacks initially subverted the established norms with an almost anarchic wit. The wit would remain, but it became politically more purposive, particularly with his move to the GDR. But as early as 1952, Hacks wrote to a school friend: "The fact, which you don't care to notice, is that the absurdities we used to appreciate earlier had a meaning as ridicule against a wrongful Nazi over-regulation (The same goes for the little tomfooleries to offset over-organised daily routines, etc.). Times have changed, though, and futility is a hallmark of everything going on these days. It is not the task of literature to make itself look ridiculous by likewise not being able to come up with anything worthwhile."

Literature should, therefore, come up with something worthwhile, which meant that it should reflect a befitting sense of artistic and social order. While reading Marx, Engels, Lenin and Brecht in the years that followed, Hacks understood how the world could be put in order. He also realised that a critical but also constructive literature could most likely be written in a socialist state. The reasons for Hacks' move to the GDR were, therefore, no less aesthetic than political. Communist art was also possible under capitalism, but not one that endorsed the social order.

In his initial years in the GDR, Hacks pursued the concept of combative, struggle-oriented literature. This may show the influence of Brecht, but in fact, it was primarily grounded in the circumstances of the time. The GDR had to fight for its survival. The border to the West was open, and particularly qualified professionals, who had been trained at great expense, were moving to the FRG, where they benefitted from the wage gap between academics and workers. In the divided city of Berlin, westerners came to the East to buy up basic necessities subsidised by the GDR state. In this situation, propaganda had an important function, and alongside dramas, Hacks wrote poetry, songs, and short agitprop plays. However, this did not correspond to his artistic ideal.

Commenting much later about Brecht and the historical context of his time, he wrote that Brecht was a classical writer who was forced by circumstances to become an enlightener. Hacks wanted to be a classical writer, and four political and economic circumstances set the stage for realising his wish. By 1960, the collectivisation of agriculture had brought about the transformation of the GDR into a socialist economy. In 1961, the GDR secured its economic independence by building the Berlin Wall. In 1963, the 'New Economic System of Planning and Management' was introduced, which intended to make the GDR economy competitive through performance incentives and led to a noticeable increase in productivity. And under Walter Ulbricht (leader of the GDR from 1949 to 1971) the state took on an independent role of reconciling conflicting but necessary forces in socialist development.

In this context, Hacks further developed his ideas of a post-revolutionary drama. Now, he was no longer concerned with a literature that would intervene directly in political struggles. The turn away from contemporary drama was also the outcome of experience: newspaper articles debated socialist development issues such as production problems. Hacks felt that drama should aim at questions that were beyond the ambit of the here and now and of day-to-day politics. Socialism, once secured, allowed (even demanded) a conception that aimed at the future. The plays that followed, mostly with historical or mythological subjects, unfolded the tension between the still inadequate present and the communist ideal that was its goal. Their purpose was not to judge the present. That the present is imperfect is a characteristic of every present. But it gained historical meaning from an inherent tendency towards the better, and that was the case in the GDR of those years.

According to Hacks, such a tendency is the basis of classical art. A classical writer does not need an ideal environment. He gains the requisite confidence by contributing to the progress of the human species in harmony with the movement of his time. His relationship to this progressive tendency is, moreover, not merely one of spontaneously going with the flow of developments, but of being intellectually infused and energised by it. The classicist, according to Hacks – and this is how he saw himself –, has become aware of the essential characteristics and questions of his time.

He also has the artistic means at his disposal to anticipate a more resplendent future and make human possibilities tangible. The use of verse in drama, impressive imagery, and compelling situations on stage could prefigure a society in which life is enjoyable. For this, the classical writer has to have a grasp of the artist's craft and knowledge of its tradition – particularly the genres, which, according to Hacks, resemble tools in which past human labour is stored that can be applied productively. The artist must, therefore, be a specialist in his subject. Hacks defended the division of labour. Communism did not stand for an austere equality but luxury for all. The task of the writer was to evoke pleasure in that ideal future. The task of the socialist state was to plan and execute the process from the still deficient socialist present towards that ideal future.

This role of the state, in particular, allowed for the emergence of a socialist classicism. Once it became apparent that socialism would be a much longer and distinct epoch on the way to communism, Walter Ulbricht fortified the role of the state in the power structure of the GDR so that it could function as an independent mediator between contending forces that were equally necessary for advancing the process of socialist development. Hacks found an analogy for this in absolutism, the period of European history during the transition from feudalism to capitalism.

In this period, characterised by a balance of power between the rising bourgeoisie and the dying feudal nobility, the king could act relatively autonomously. He first progressively promoted the bourgeoisie, which brought him tax revenues with which he could rise above other feudal lords. The more powerful the bourgeoisie became, the more reactionary absolutism had to become because the king relied increasingly on the nobility to stave off a bourgeois revolution. In the long run, the absolutist equilibrium proved to be unsustainable. However, it is the period of equilibrium that interested Hacks.

In the GDR, too, he saw two contending social forces. On the one hand, there was the party, which rightly tried to enforce social equality: the desired future. On the other hand, there were the specialists required for a functioning economy who stood for the idea of quality and performance with just as good reasons: the need of the present. The state had to mediate between these forces to promote socialist development. For Hacks, this balancing function of the socialist state was epitomised in the figure of Walter Ulbricht. Accordingly, the ideal hero of his dramas was the hero in the middle. Being in the middle did not mean a compromise between the contending groups but a position above them that had the whole picture in mind.

The choice of genre connected with this conception. Most of Hacks' plays are comedies. Admittedly, this decision is not just theoretically grounded: even the earliest surviving texts testify to his preference for humour, including jokes. But the GDR, with its non-antagonistic contradictions, offered the ideal basis for treating conflicts seriously in a comic way. There's always plenty to laugh about in his works, even in the one drama that he labeled a 'tragedy'. The plots almost always end with the most important conflicts resolved or at least set aside. However, this is sometimes accompanied by a sad moment: in a world that is not perfect, it is not possible to balance the contradictions without losses for the individual. The comedies, light as many of them come across, thus incorporate tragic elements.

This is a kind of ideal version of Hacksian aesthetics, and what he wrote in the thirty years of his life after Ulbricht's fall in 1971 is characterised by an attempt to maintain under new circumstances the height he had reached in the 1960s and to productively use the aesthetic means he had worked out. Outwardly, the new era under Erich Honecker was off to a good start. In 1971, Honecker proclaimed that if one proceeds from the firm position of socialism, there should be no taboos in the field of art and literature. In fact, Hacks had it easier under Honecker than under Ulbricht. Now his dramas were frequently performed. But Hacks was less concerned with his own success than with the development of the socialist state. Under Honecker, the party, which wanted to distribute wealth, gained the upper hand over the specialists whose task was to generate wealth. The equilibrium was lost. For Hacks, this meant a departure from the requirements of a socialist economy in an imperialist environment. For a short time, there were more consumer goods in the GDR, but the result was indebtedness to capitalist countries and then all the greater misery.

CRITIQUE OF ROMANTICISM

The poem '1.8.1973' in this volume shows that Hacks recognised the dangers associated with this policy early on. The poem could not be printed in the GDR for a long time. Such problems did not shake Hacks' basic commitment to socialism and the GDR. He was not against censorship in socialism at all, but only against stupid censorship. He understood quite well why younger authors took positions different from his; the note in this volume about young writers in the GDR shows this. At the same time, he resolutely disapproved of an opposition in the GDR that saw itself as left-wing and criticised the shortcomings in the existing system from the perspective of a communist utopia. This utopianism meant destroying the tension between the possible and the desired, substituting subjective complaints for political analysis.

In the 1960s, Hacks saw himself as a representative of art in a period of socialist awakening. In the decades that followed, he found himself more and more on the defensive. Accordingly, there is much more polemics in the essay writing of that time. Hacks still saw himself as a classicist, but now his focus shifted to a critique of romanticism. German romanticism, described by its influential representative Friedrich Schlegel as a 'progressive universal poesy', was the contemporary counter-model to classicism, of which Goethe was the main representative. Early romanticism from around 1790 was sceptical about the possibility of understanding the world rationally, which was reflected in ironic and subjectivist attitudes. Its aesthetics emphasised the fragmentary instead of the completed work, and mixed forms instead of the genre with its rules. Philosophically, its accent was on the particular instead of the whole. This prompted its later turn to nationalism and its opposition to Napoleon and to a state that stood for progress in Germany after 1806. With this historical reference, Hacks also expressed his disapproval of those GDR authors who seized a romantic aesthetics to criticise their state.

Politically, this meant that Hacks lost the bonus he had enjoyed as an occasionally banned author – in West Germany in any case, and in the East in artistic circles. It was now clear that he was not hoping for the liberalisation of the GDR. On the contrary, he wrote: "One can live with the party. My wish, were I to have a right, / would be, that it be a little more partisan."

His interest in Stalin dates from this phase. He saw Stalin as a strategically astute leader who was able to maintain and develop the Soviet Union under the hostile conditions of imperialism. This was precisely because Stalin never had illusions about imperialism's willingness for peace. At home, Stalin kept two extreme political positions at bay: on the one hand, those who were in favour of the market and liberalisation, and on the other, those who immediately demanded communism and world revolution without thinking about the preconditions. Stalin thus represented the qualities that Hacks missed both in the GDR leadership under Honecker and in the left-wing opposition. After the end of the GDR, Hacks saw Stalin and Lenin as communist leaders who understood the need to maintain a strong state as a bulwark against imperialism and as a condition for the future of socialism.

Aesthetically, the classicist Hacks became a post-classicist in the late phase of the GDR without changing his basic positions.

The playwright no longer stood above contending viewpoints but had to take a side himself.

THE STATE AND IMPERIALISM

At times, drama took a back seat in the fight against opportunism, and with it, the essay became the focus of his work. Hacks realised that socialism was under threat. In these writings, his focus was not so much on imperialism, which had existed through the 20th century, but on the flagging will to defend what had been achieved under socialism. After the GDR was annexed to the FRG, he wrote several political poems, which he published in some left-wing magazines. Hacks continued to use jokes as an aesthetic means. But the jokes became more and more polemical and sarcastic.

After 1989/90, Hacks consistently and intentionally took on an outsider position. He left unanswered the many interview requests from major bourgeois newspapers, particularly after the publication of his essays. He wanted to have as little to do with the unified Germany, which he saw as imperialist, as with its journalist minions. He preferred to publish in marginal magazines and publishing houses. He refused to criticise the GDR, which would have opened the way back for him to recognition in the mainstream.

In the peak period of his classical works, Hacks had been concerned with the prospects of an apparently secure GDR; the state in the GDR had stood for historical progress, even though he had become increasingly critical of it in its final decade. After 1989, he found himself in a state he rejected. The enlarged FRG was, for him, part of a historically outdated, albeit still destructively powerful imperialism. From the 1980s, particularly after the collapse of socialism, the struggle against imperialism by states in the outside world took centre stage in his plays. The plays he wrote in this period are, in the main, shorter and no longer in verse. Though still classical in their conception and set in the past, they are moved, for instance, by the struggle in post-Soviet Russia against rulers installed by the West, the threats faced by China from the West and the US-led war on Iraq.

ABOUT THE SELECTION IN THIS VOLUME

This volume brings together translations by the editors and those already published in the volume *On Imperialism, Socialism, and the Responsibility of the Artist*, brought out by Perspektive Internationale in 2020, with translations by Michael Dorrity. The 2020 volume was aimed mainly at introducing Hacks as a political writer and was also translated into Spanish. It included essays, short commentaries, interviews, and poems that were selected for this purpose. Several of the essays, shorter comments and interviews are from Hacks' *Marxistische Hinsichten: Politische Schriften 1955–2003* (Marxist Perspectives: Political Writings 1955 – 2003), which brings together much of his specifically political responses and reflections. The volume also included some essays under the heading 'Art and Revolution' as also a number of poems. This collection was the starting point for the present volume. We have essentially expanded it and edited the translations in consultation with Michael Dorrity to harmonise them with the new translations.

The general aim of the present volume is to introduce Peter Hacks to a larger audience. LeftWord Books provides enviable access to readers who may find interest in a writer such as Hacks, not least because of his political views. While introducing Hacks to such an audience, the editors also had the following considerations in mind. Firstly, to make the collection more representative of his writings. Secondly, to also specifically include pieces that represent Hacks' aesthetic ideas. As has been highlighted above, the political and aesthetic facets of his writing are not separate but intimately connected; however, it needs to be emphasised that Peter Hacks was primarily an artist who sought in socialism the fertile environment suited to his artistic inclinations. We have therefore added a few of his essays and excerpts from other longer ones, in which he formulates his views on art, theatre, the importance of form in general and genres in particular and the depravity of the media. All his essays are written in an inimitable and provocative style, and whether you always agree with him or not, they are a pleasure to read and an incitement to set you thinking.

It needs to be mentioned that though Hacks was first and foremost a playwright, this volume includes only one play, and that too, a very short one, which the author called a playlet. Hacks' plays, of which there are no less than fifty, are not easy to translate, particularly since many of them are written in verse. There are also allusions to German history that present a further challenge to any translator. The formidable task of translating his major plays will, therefore, have to wait. But the playlet included in this volume is interesting on two counts. 'The Bishop of China', as suggested by the title, is set in China. It is based on a historical event. Though set in the 18th century, its allusions to contemporary times are evident and make for mightily amusing reading. It was also one of the last plays written by Hacks in which his focus is on the conflicts with imperialism in other parts of the world.

Hacks' publications in German include two volumes of anecdotes, one written by Hacks alone, the other in collaboration with fellow writer and friend, André Müller. The anecdotes are about Hacks and express in inventive and humorous ways his approach to the world in which he lived. This volume includes twenty anecdotes from the first volume and eighteen from the second. Apart from the short anecdote, Hacks also wrote several other short emblematic pieces that are strewn in his writings. A few of them are also included, such as the closing piece entitled 'Autobiography.'

Hacks' poems have a wide range of themes: political, historical, art, nature and love. Unlike most contemporary poetry, Hacks' poems are, for the most part, in rhyme and span a range from longer poems to couplets and distichs. The poems that appear in this volume offer a flavour of the themes and forms as well as changes in mood in response to changes in the political environment. We wish to thank Dirk Wiemann for his insightful suggestions that improved the translations of several poems.

Writing for children constitutes three volumes of Hacks' works published in 15 volumes, the first of poems and plays, the second of what might be called fantastic tales and the third of novels. Novels for children were the only novels he wrote. This volume includes a few poems, a fantastic tale and a very short story to give an idea of the nature of the literary investment Hacks made in children, in whom he saw the potential for becoming emancipated individuals in the future.

Besides the novels and fantastic tales for children, Hacks also wrote several longer and shorter stories. We have included a few of the shorter and still shorter ones.

Although a few translations of Peter Hacks into English exist, they are not available in print and are difficult to access. Many more translations were done into Russian, other East and West European languages, and some also into Chinese, Japanese and Korean. Translating Hacks is, as mentioned earlier, far from easy. His poems are mostly in rhyme, the translations of which we approached with great trepidation, though also with doggedness. Moreover, apart from the historical and political references, his prose writing and his plays are characterised every so often by a resort to neologisms, a deliberate choice of words that are old-fashioned or no longer in use and a tendency to sometimes use rhyming words or words related grammatically or semantically. Finding adequate translations for such instances often took quite a while, all the more so since what works in German often doesn't work in English. It is for the readers to judge whether the translations read well while also conveying the writer's idiosyncratic turn of phrase. Hacks' formulations also include a few instances where the meaning appears to be cryptic. They are part of his style, so we have not tried to make them clearer in the translation than they are in the original. Titles in brackets are titles not given by Hacks.

A Persons Index has been provided at the end of the volume for the numerous names of historical and literary figures that appear in Hacks' writings. A list of abbreviations used by Hacks appears at the beginning. Footnotes have been added wherever necessary.

This anthology is the outcome of a collaborative project. The editors wish to thank Florentine Morales Sandoval from the Perspektive Internationale for initiating it. Special thanks are due to Perspektive Internationale and Michael Dorrity for allowing us to include their translations. We wish to further thank the International Union of Left Publishers and LeftWord Books, in particular, for opening the doors to the project. Thanks to Devi Vijay for her careful editing and suggestions to improve the text. Our thanks also go to the Peter Hacks Society and Eulenspiegel Verlag (Berlin), the publishers of Hacks' works, for granting the rights to translate and publish the pieces included in this volume. The anthology includes only a very small selection from Hacks' oeuvre. We hope, nevertheless, that it will give readers a flavour of the work of this extraordinary and engaging writer who is still waiting to be discovered.

Shaswati Mazumdar	Kai Köhler
Delhi	Berlin

(Auto-)biographical

Personal Particulars

1.

P.H. was born in 1928 and belongs to that cohort that was encouraged by the smashing of German fascism and the founding of the GDR to put hope in the course of the world. He is a writer; his life contains no external events.

2.

Apart from and assuming his wife Anna Elisabeth Wiede, P.H. has loved three women: Eva Maria Hagen, Sibylle Belicke and Karin Gregorek. Other women may put forth much more and far more convincing written evidence of his affection, but he did not love other women.

3.

P.H. was friends with André Müller.[1]

4.

In literary terms, P.H. may be classified as follows. The first half of the century belongs to Thomas Mann and Bertolt Brecht, the second belongs to him and Arno Schmidt (The left bourgeoisie is responsible for German prose, and communism for drama and poetry).[2] P.H. differs from the other three named in that his poetry

1 André Müller (1925–2021), West German communist. Trained as a carpenter and self-taught theatre critic who was a founder of the Arbeitskreis Bertolt Brecht, a working group set up in 1957 to engage with the work of Bertolt Brecht in West Germany. He was editor of its newsletter and later of the DKP-affiliated magazine "Kultur & Gesellschaft" (Culture & Society). Müller's own work includes two novels, several short stories and plays, collections of anecdotes about Marx, Brecht and Hacks, among others, as well as studies of Shakespeare's dramas in two volumes. He had a close friendship with Hacks for a good four decades. Especially in the last twenty years of his life, Müller was the most important conversation partner for Hacks, which is documented in an extensive correspondence and in the records of the conversations later published by Müller.

2 Thomas Mann (1875–1955) and Arno Schmidt (1914–1979) were German novelists, whose writing Hacks admired and whom he saw as left-wing but not communist.

is not only good but also right in terms of content and requires no excuse at all.

5.

Politically, he is an Ulbrichtian, a supporter of enlightened and still-to-be-illuminated Stalinism. He considers Ulbricht's system to be the appropriate practice for adapting Stalin's production relations to the advancing production forces; he considers the feasibility of this practice to have been tried out and proven in the GDR reality of the 1960s.

6.

The decline and ultimate collapse of socialism occurred during his lifetime. This shifted him from the position of the classical author to the less favourable position of a post-classic, but did not lead him to the opinion that Hegel had described things wrongly.

7.

The establishment of socialism in one country was a highly risky venture. Not because socialism could not have developed in underdeveloped Russia, but rather because it had the bulk of the developed countries as tireless enemies. In spite of this, P.H. believes that the project could have been sustained; incidentally, he still does not see how one could have refrained from making the Russian Revolution.

8.

P.H. does not claim to have given the world a philosophy. His thinking is based on the existing state of knowledge of mankind; he finds its content described in the complete works of the following eight thinking and acting people: Goethe, Hegel, Marx, Engels, Lenin, Stalin, Ulbricht, Andropov.

9.

P.H. is the Stalinist of the playhouse.

[around 2000]

Anecdotes by Hacks

MAXIM

The composer Baby Faber took some interest in Hacks in his early years in Munich, and also recounted to him a number of episodes and experiences.

As the Nazis increasingly turned to the business of race, Faber had found it advisable to seek shelter for a while in a psychiatric clinic. The doctors there took the artist for a harmless madman, but the idiots themselves, according to Faber, were incredibly kind to him.

They cosseted me, as he described it, they led me to the piano, they made me sit down on the stool and listened to my recital. And then they sang along, and how they sang along! My life among the lunatics, he recapitulated; basically, it was the best time of my life.

Everyone laughed. Hacks thought to himself for a moment.

My life among the lunatics, he repeated, would you consider gifting me that line?

Sure, said the musician, but what for?

I could be at a loss someday for a motto for my lifetime, said the precocious student.

A BEGINNING

Hacks, who at that time was still a man full of hope and of little action, wrote to Brecht, whom he revered above all else and asked whether he would recommend moving his residence from Munich to the GDR. Brecht urgently advised him against it, and Hacks betook himself to the GDR.

It was the first time, says Hacks, that I showed more sense than Brecht.

A SMALL REQUEST

Brecht asked the writer Anna Elisabeth Wiede and Peter Hacks to translate the Irish comedy "The Playboy of The Western World" by J.M. Synge for his theatre. He believed it was a very poetic text that could be written down quickly in a few days. After a month, Wiede and Hacks turned up and said they had brought the first act.

Already? said Brecht, quite astonished.

AN UNCOMMON EXPRESSION

Whether the talk is about Emperor Nero, Duke Carl August of Weimar, or Walter Ulbricht, Hacks absolutely refuses to regard the state as such as evil. He quite likes to use the term state humanism, although it is not a commonly used expression.

What I designate as state humanism, says Hacks, is the opinion that the goal of history is the development of the individual and that the state is the appropriate lever to push through the development of the individual on a mass scale.

THE ELEVENTH THESIS ON DIRECTOR'S THEATRE

Hacks dispensed with the degraded theatre of the last quarter of the century by dint of a withering phrase that will one day be affixed in bronze letters to the marble wall of the Academy of Performing Arts.

"Directors have only changed the plays in various ways, the point is to interpret them".

MATERIALISM

For a few years, Hacks acted as a mentor to the Circle of Working Class Writers in Hagenauer Street. The founders of the circle were the veterans Bruno and Emmi Jacob. Emmi had been a courier for Rosa Luxemburg, and Bruno wrote the poem: 'What does the skylark sing with esprit? Joliot Curie, Joliot Curie!' The other participants were also writers, but by no means workers. Friends asked Hacks what kind of material recognition the concerned municipality gave for his work.

I've been successful in my fight for the right to the most comfortable chair available, the poet informed them, that much material recognition is enough for me.

DÉJÀ VU

Anna Wiede and Peter Hacks often travelled to Tito's Yugoslavia, sometimes together with James Krüss, sometimes alone. For Hacks, Belgrade was the first city he saw in his life adorned with red flags. On the next trip, there were no more red flags to be seen; instead, pictures as high as houses of the American President were hanging from the roof gutters.

I've seen all of this before, Hacks said in 1990 in the face of the turnaround in Berlin, but you don't think anything like that could ever happen in your own capital.

HACKS' LIMITATION

You're not a Europe-centrist, are you? asked a man of advanced principles suspiciously.

Let me think, Hacks responded. The westernmost point I've ever been to is Versailles. The northernmost is Hiddensee, the easternmost is Yerevan and, by the way, it is also the southernmost, because Yerevan is two degrees of latitude closer to the equator than Dubrovnik, which would otherwise occupy this final position.

But it doesn't change anything, Hacks concluded; it's all come out now; I'm a proven GDR centrist and absolutely unable to deny it.

THE POINTLESSNESS OF CATASTROPHES

Hacks, whose temperament attached importance to the reliability of basic facts, had settled in Brandenburg because one did not have to reckon with earthquakes, volcanic eruptions and catastrophic floods there. When the Notte rose above its banks in the great flood of 2002 and the hurricane tore the old oak trees in the park from their foundations, a sympathetic friend called him.

How are things with you? said the friend.

Ah, Hacks complained, awful.

Is the damage extensive? said the friend.

Any damage is limited in some way or the other, Hacks said. What's unbearable about the whole thing is that it is a thoroughly superfluous natural phenomenon. There's nothing to be thought about it, even with the best will in the world.

IN DEFENCE OF THE MEASURES

A communist who had been cured of cancer summed up his experience in the following complaint: The cancer doesn't hurt, only the measures against the cancer do.

Don't talk reformist rubbish, Hacks admonished. Your criticism is no more valid than if you had said: capitalism does not hurt, only the measures against capitalism do. And he added:

The point is not whether the measures hurt, but only whether they are the right ones.

COWARDICE AND DRAMA

Hacks thought highly of two of his country's playwrights, Rudi Strahl and Helmut Baierl. What he liked about them was that they each tackled GDR problems in their own unique way, neither as imitators of the Russian or Brechtian communists, nor as slaves of fashion and the foreign. The fact that, apart from having quite a few good ideas, neither of them had been able to produce any work of lasting value, he imputed to their lack of courage rather than lack of talent. Strahl, he said, submits to the theatre audience, Baierl to the theatre management floors. And he said:

They remind me of wolf mothers who send their well-built whelps to the school for bunny rabbits for further training.

MOMENT OF CONTEMPLATION

Hacks, who was always punctual, showed up two minutes late for a meal with his colleague Jochen Berg. I beg your indulgence, he said, I was thinking about my imperfections.

You didn't spend a lot of time on it, remarked Berg.

No, said Hacks, but I think very fast.

PREREQUISITE FOR AN AWARD

Hacks was listening to a conversation about the Provençal poet Frédéric Mistral. Mistral, said Hacks, butting into the conversation, wasn't he that child of nature who intuitively realised that, despite all requisite sympathy for revolutions, one had to clearly distance oneself from the excesses of revolutions if one wanted to win the Nobel Prize?

And before anyone could reply, he continued:

It's required for the Nobel Prize, but I must add right away that it's also enough for the Nobel Prize.

LANDSCAPES WITHOUT FRILLS

Those who defeated Helmut Kohl in the elections liked to refer to the ex-chancellor as the biggest liar because he had promised the GDR citizens "blooming landscapes".

Hacks defended Kohl against such mobbing. You can't be more honest than this politician, he said. Did he ever use a single word that implied "cheerful people"?

NICOLAIVIERTEL, BERLIN

It is generally believed that imperialism will make the world uninhabitable by its wars.

Hacks stepped out of a steakhouse with friends. It was a beautiful summer night, they had enjoyed the meal and were now enjoying the view.

The moon, the river Spree, the Engelhardt monument, said Hacks, I'll bet on it, if we let the imperialists carry on for another ten years, they'll get rid of them too. They'll bring this off even without bombs.

GORBACHEV

It seems a bit peevish, Hacks remarked about Gorbachev's criticism of Stalin, when a notorious loser accuses a notorious winner of bad politics.

But he didn't want to hold Gorbachev solely responsible for the downfall of the communist occident:

Gorbachevism is only the concluding passage of the destruction of reason.

PRESUMPTUOUS FREEDOM FIGHTERS

Hacks heard the French philosopher Glucksman railing against Stalin on television and was infuriated. These loudmouth media rabble, he grumbled, hold it personally against Stalin that he would have, as they like to imagine, killed all of them in Siberia for their opinions. This assumption is absurd; had they lived under Stalin's rule, they would have flattered and worshipped him just as uninhibitedly as they now flatter and worship the bourgeoisie. It's they, in fact, who would have been absolutely safe from him.

FRAUDULENT LABELLING

There was agreement that the Federal Republic was no longer an "industrial society", but what kind of society was it? Some said, a services society, others an information society.

"I hate to choose between those two definitions", said Hacks when he was asked, "since in our imperialist Germany, it is equally impossible to either get any service or any information."

URBAN PLANNING

After the attack on the two skyscrapers on Manhattan Island, known as the 'Centre of World Trade', Hacks asked Klaus Steiniger, who was more adept in the ins and outs of life, if he saw himself in a position to help him get the postal address of the graduate engineer Osama bin Laden. By way of explanation, he wrote that he had some urgent matters to discuss with the same about the redesigning of Potsdamer Platz.

OPTIMISM DEBATE

Can one do anything at all? said a fellow fighter who was fed up.
Aren't we doing anything? Hacks asked.
Whatever we do, said the friend, it doesn't yield any results.
Who knows, said Hacks. Today none, tomorrow sure enough.

[around 2000]

Anecdotes by André Müller[3] in Collaboration with Hacks

IN DEFENCE OF BRECHT

Hacks regarded Brecht highly as a writer, but was often critical of his work, since most of the modern stupidities of art can be derived from or given sanction by him. This earned him the reputation of being hostile to Brecht.

A friend who shared these opinions pointed out, however, that it was becoming fashionable to attack Brecht and that it would soon be necessary to defend him.

Yes, Hacks agreed, the following groups of people do not have the prerogative of criticising Brecht:

1. those who do not honestly know and follow Marx's teachings,

2. those who do not support or produce realistic theatre in an outstanding manner, and

3. those who haven't read Brecht

I'm really keen to know who's left.

HARMFUL POEMS

The Claassen publishing house in Düsseldorf had committed to publishing a collection of poems by Hacks. As he looked through them, the editor, a born romantic, began to hesitate. He found the poems too classical, too artistic, too communist, and therefore not revolutionary enough.

"Believe me," he urged Hacks, "publishing these poems will be harmful for you here."

It doesn't matter, Hacks replied, if I follow my critics in both German states, everything I've ever written is harmful for me.

3 See Fn 2.

CUSTOM

When the West German Chancellor Willy Brandt and the Minister President of the GDR Willi Stoph met in Erfurt in 1970, there was much discussion in Berlin as to the reasons that led Ulbricht to agree to such a meeting or even bring it about.

Hacks also wondered: Is he pacifying the Russians to show that he supports their policy of detente, or does he want to demonstrate to them his independence in German politics?

Neither of the two views could be agreed upon. One interlocutor therefore suggested that maybe there was no reason at all.

Nonsense, Hacks said dismissively. Intercourse in public always takes place with some objectives in mind.

NEW IDEA

After visiting a performance of Brecht's parable 'The Good Person of Sezuan', in which the good-natured prostitute Shen Te has to transform into the evil cousin Shui Ta in order to survive in the world, Hacks found new interest in the parable and was more taken by this work of Brecht than before.

The play is more realistic than I thought, he remarked in earnest on the way home, and it can inspire sequels, for example, a prologue: Lenin, faced with the need to take particularly unpopular measures, stages his death in the Kremlin and continues to govern in the mask of Stalin.

DANGEROUS TIMES

At the time when the APO, the extra-parliamentary opposition, was having its heyday in the Federal Republic and West Berlin, Hacks foresaw with disquiet the end of the epoch of art in the GDR. He feared that the APO's views on art, appearing as they did in Marxist costume, could infiltrate unhindered into the GDR, whose art bureaucracy was incapable of seeing through this.

There is an unmistakable sign that things are starting to

change, he explained to a visitor. I hear even I shall be officially allowed in the future.

ASSESSMENT

A theatre magazine indulged in the favourite pastime of all editors. It conducted a survey, this time among playwrights, to see whether they could live on the income from their plays.

All those who were asked complained to a greater or lesser extent that they earned too little and that it was impossible to make a living from writing plays. Hacks was the exception.

Better than I thought, he replied, but of course worse than what's beseeming.

LOFTY PIQUE

Hacks had given the children's book publisher a manuscript of children's poems. There was no response from the publisher for a quarter of a year, then he sent Hacks a list of 18 proposed changes, which editors commonly use to prove their right to exist. Another quarter of a year later, there came an enquiry as to why Hacks had not commented on the list.

It was naturally of great private interest to me, Hacks wrote back, to know what book you would have written if you could have written it.

After another three months, the children's poems appeared just as Hacks had composed them.

A SMALL ERROR

After Ulbricht's fall, which Honecker could only bring about with Soviet help, like-minded people debated with Hacks what the Soviet Union actually wanted.

Sugar and spice and all things nice, Hacks explained. They've actually started to believe that if they're peaceful, friendly, and accommodating, then imperialism would be too.

TV DELIGHTS

Hacks watched a television documentary about McCarthy's fall and his desperate fightback, his last hopes, and his ultimate downfall. Hacks appreciated such shows immensely and claimed that he didn't really know anything more fascinating.

McCarthy was an ace villain, he declared, his counterattacks to prevent his fall were masterful, and what one learns from this film is: nothing whatsoever will help you once you have been condemned by a society, in this case, not even the otherwise so potent communist danger."

An acquaintance who had seen the film wanted to know why McCarthy had actually been toppled, after all he was a first-class anti-communist and wasn't anti-communism so very popular in the USA?

Hacks replied, In the end, not one administrative department or post office functioned anymore because he suspected every single one of them of communism. McCarthy was just too good.

LAST FLASH

An acquaintance from the West visited Hacks at his country house in the marshlands. He drove his Western car in the direction of Königs Wusterhausen, stopping on the way to buy flowers for the lady of the house. As he was about to get back into his car, he noticed that his front tire had been punctured. He changed the tire to the taunts of a group of young hooligans and hence arrived late at Hacks' place.

After he had cleaned himself up, he reported the reason for his late arrival and expressed the view that the youngsters had probably been the perpetrators and had done so because he was driving a car with a Western license plate.

It may well be, Hacks answered sympathetically. Unlike Honecker, our young people are still waging the class struggle.

STRICTLY CONSERVATIVE

During a discussion, the subject came up of teaching girls and boys together in one class, as had been the general rule in the GDR. To the amazement of almost everyone, Hacks opposed this principle of education and insisted on separate classes and schools according to sex.

However, he added, the girls' and boys' schools should always be right next to each other and, as a matter of principle, have high walls between them overgrown with ivy so that one can easily clamber over. Public conveniences should also be there, with enough knotholes in the branches. In this way, curiosity about the opposite sex can develop and be sustained, otherwise I'd like to see how many repressed individuals there'll be in thirty years.

FRUSTRATION

In the mid-1980s, a Korean airliner was shot down over the territory of the USSR when it refused a landing request from Soviet fighter pilots. The incident was used for a massive anti-Soviet campaign, although numerous facts indicated that it was a deliberate provocation by agencies of the US, in which the loss of the passenger plane had been consciously taken into account.

However, it took the Soviet authorities four days to even admit the downing and hint at the true facts. By this time, world opinion had long since been hammered out in accordance with American views.

Infuriated by the loss of time, Hacks said, It's as if I slapped a member of the Politburo, who then consulted at all possible levels for four days before deciding to slap me back! Really, the Russians act as if they've been caught masturbating.

CONCLUSION

The SED, or what was left of it, morphed after the end of the GDR into the PDS, which decided to completely abandon Marxism but allowed individual members to continue dreaming of it.

In order to explain its behaviour, it even fell back on Marxism and claimed that the attempt to introduce socialism in individual nation states had also failed because socialism conceived nationally did not work – the national idea is supposedly a contradiction to the internationalism conclusively demonstrated by Marx.

That's a familiar refrain, Hacks said. Idiots always grasp any new truth in such an abstract way that it becomes impracticable. In this case, on purpose.

HUMBLE QUESTION

After the fall of the GDR, it became fashionable in the PDS to present the October Revolution of 1917 as the final and decisive reason for its end: capitalism was not yet ripe for its downfall, the development of socialism in one country had inevitably led to disfigurements, these were inherited by the other countries, and that subsequently led to their demise.

Hacks remained sceptical: This view plainly excuses all those who led the GDR astray, ruined it and toppled it, and it also excuses international monopoly capital for having spent billions to overthrow socialism, he said. But if we leave that aside: Can someone perhaps tell me how the October Revolution could have been prevented?

LOYALTY TO ONESELF

After Honecker was deposed as party chief of the SED, he spoke in a survey about the reasons that he believed led to the fall of the GDR. During a conversation, someone who was not familiar with these statements asked Hacks what Honecker had said.

He said unequivocally that Gorbachev had abolished world socialism, Hacks reported. But Honecker also said that he is still proud of having contributed to Helsinki[4], the House of Europe and

4 Helsinki Accords, signed in 1975 at the end of the Conference on Security and Co-operation in Europe held in Helsinki, Finland, as a step towards detente between the Eastern socialist and Western capitalist blocs.

the whole show of trust. In short, he happily proclaimed himself an opportunist, but was aggrieved by the fact that capitalism had triumphed over opportunism.

ENVY

When Brecht's diaries from the period of emigration appeared, Hacks read them right away and very carefully.

There is nothing new to say about his art, he informed the editor, Brecht only knows enlightenment. But politically he's almost always at his best, which really can't be said of Thomas Mann. I found a sentence in Brecht that belongs in every Marxist treasure chest: Dictatorships always conceal the economic character of violence and democracies always the violent character of the economy.

He added enviously: I would have liked to have written that sentence.

HISTORICAL LESSONS

The workers of France were once again on strike and creating quite a stir. They occupied factories, paralysed all traffic, acted as if they were ready for violence and invincible, even unsettling the neighbouring country with all this.

The romantic left spoke enthusiastically of a revolution. Hacks remained sceptical.

It will all come to nothing, he predicted. In general, the workers of France have a marvellous talent for starting revolutions in order to lose them.

FINAL WORD

A lady taking part in a conversation revealed that she was one of those people who had a heart of gold, who only did good and wished no one any harm.

"But I beg you," Hacks pleaded, "please don't count me among them."

Political

[1962]

Letter to the German-African Society

German-African Society
Berlin

Dear Sirs,

We would be very happy if you would consider it right to accept us as members of the German-African Society. We take a strong interest in the anti-imperialist struggle of the African peoples, and we show this interest through literary works, of which we would like to mention Wiede's play in the making on Lumumba and Hacks' songs (Save Ben Bella, Freedom for Gisenga, Lumumba's Death). Enclosed: endorsements of this application by Dr. Schmaus and Claus Küchenmeister.

We are, with kind regards,

Anna Elisabeth Wiede   Dr. Peter Hacks

[24. 12. 1965]

On the War of Aggression in Vietnam

1

The entire Vietnam has been split into three parts. The north is under socialist people's rule, the south governed by a coalition of independent and democratic groups. One fifth of the south, i.e. a tenth of the entire territory, is ruled by the American military, assisted by Vietnamese non-volunteers and some contract killers of varying nationalities. These forces have attacked Vietnam. They are currently going about subjugating the country or, given that such efforts have been frustrated by the heroic resistance of the liberation army, hoping at least to exterminate its people, regardless of which of the three parts they belong to.

2

For a time, the US government had insisted that they were fighting this war in the interest of their few political whores in Saigon. The laughable absurdity of this claim was obvious; by definition, a whore has no interests of her own. The US government later issued a different reason for the war: protection of American interests. These interests are essentially those of the foreign and domestic market. It is common knowledge, after all, that there scarcely exists a serious business in modern capitalism that does not make use of violence. The Americans, who under certain conditions might be willing to forego the exploitative bondage common under classical or political colonialism, would not for a moment consider denying themselves the fruits of neo-colonial exploitation which is more profitable and more demeaning still. It is precisely from this kind of exploitation that Vietnam had freed itself, with Asia determined to do the same. What's more, the US government, like all state capitalist governments, is tasked with the forced sale of certain useless industrial products to its own population. Before all these highly expensive armaments end up decaying on the bloody scrap heap of Vietnam, they must first be paid for by the American taxpayer, whose opinion on the matter goes quite unsolicited. These interests are, as such, those of a class of Americans who are more influential than they are numerous. It seems, however, that these interests conflict with those of too many others to be able to claim any special recognition.

3

A small nation, which anxiously attends to its own productivity, has been attacked by a large, rich one. The havoc wreaked by the latter is almost indescribable. There is no known infernality that it does not commit. It is not content with killing the local people; the very unborn are pursued for decades. Houses are burned, vegetation poisoned, workshops laid bare, paths blown up, water supplies ruptured. This invading nation forms an alliance with humanity's oldest enemies; epidemics. For nothing more than money, it wages a war that verges on world war and creates a hell that verges on hell on earth.

4

Writers put aside their projects for the future of the earth and observe this American project with anger. It bears little resemblance to the best possible condition of the human race which they had imagined. Wherever they live, whatever their ideas, they feel compelled, with what tools they have, to stop its execution. This stance has no bearing on the debate as to whether writers should concern themselves with politics, their decision has nothing to do with the question of political partisanship. This is a decision within the literary field itself, for the writer's vocation is that of human dignity. In Vietnam, the rights they advocate are stifled under the impact of explosives, poison and gas. The poet's calling is anti-imperialist.

5

In light of this, the German PEN Centre issues the following declaration: we must make clear to the powerful in the US that the times when a human being could be treated as a mere object like any other, to be sawed, chopped and smashed at one's discretion, are coming to an end. This is the most abhorrent political crime since Hitler, and it must be prosecuted and punished. We must do everything to hinder America's war and to assist the Vietnamese people.

6

The German PEN Centre opposes all attitudes of obfuscating congeniality, all halving of guilt or responsibility. It opposes all those who would take into account that the USA cannot afford to lose face. Are we to believe President Johnson? Believe that this heartless, calculating robotic grimace is the face of America? Even America, that island on the far side of world culture, neglected by history and poorly favoured by progress, even America has other faces. One of the most noble is that of the coloured and white civil rights campaigners, students and professors, threatened by state police, fascist mobs and blacklists. With the greatest of courage, they say what is said here. Even America is home to human beings, even America's true face is human.

7

The German PEN Centre (East and West) calls on the PEN Centres of the Federal Republic, the US, all other local and national Centres, and the international PEN Centre in particular, to endorse this statement, in letter or spirit.

[Draft for a PEN-declaration]

"A Revolution Against the State?" Questions in the Title and Seven Others[5]

Question 1: Do you believe that changes in politics and society should only be brought about within the framework of existing political arrangements as guaranteed by our constitution?

Dear Mr. Dollinger, at first I actually thought you were referring to me. You're investigating, it is clear from the title of your survey, the intentions of the German Left, and I certainly belong to the German Left. It became clear to me some time later, however, that your use of the word German is quite peculiar, namely in place of West German. You actually mean the West German Left, to which I just as certainly do not belong. Of course, anyone would be flattered to be asked for his advice on the concerns of others. I am as much susceptible to flattery as anyone else, which is why I am replying to you so eagerly.

There is, incidentally, yet another allure to your questions that I find rather appealing, by which I mean their overrefined obscurity and the fact that they are so difficult to decipher. You do not call things by the names used by the authors of the Marxist classics, and which were customary in the language of the eighteenth and nineteenth century. Nor do you think in the same fashion as those whom you address. Or perhaps when you say the Left, you do not

5 The Munich publicist Hans Dollinger wrote to several writers including Hacks for a contribution to a book on the APO in West Germany with the title "Revolution against the state?". His letter contained seven questions. Hacks referred to it in a letter to his mother: "Mr. Dollinger from Munich sent me a very progressive questionnaire, which boils down to the problem of what can be done for a revolution, so that it is bound not to happen." In his response to Dollinger Hacks also addressed the question in the title before answering the seven questions which he also reformulated. The questions (in italics) are taken from Dollinger's book (*Revolution gegen den Staat? Die außerparlamentarische Opposition – die neue Linke. Eine politische Anthologie*. hg. von Hans Dollinger. Bern-München-Wien 1968).

mean the Left at all? When one refers to the Left in plain language, one usually means the social group that endeavours to change unproductive property relations, that is to say, for the last one hundred years or so, the Marxists. Why then do you ask the Left the question "revolution against the state"? This question comes from Eugen Dühring, not Karl Marx.

As far as I can see, there is a dire need to overthrow monopoly capital in the FRG. Such an undertaking is, of course, also aimed at the monopoly-capitalist state. But the state is not (as Eugen Dühring tells us) the original force of domination. Rather, it is economic domination (as Karl Marx tells us) from which political domination is derived. You are then, at the least, imprecise enough as to mistake the appearance of evil for its essence. But you do not even ask, how I wish you would, about the monopoly-capitalist state, you ask only about the state as such. There are as many answers to that question as there are states. As long as the North Americans, for example, make use of a state, it is not so easy to see how the Cubans, for example, are supposed to do without one.

As such, I shall take the occasional liberty to translate your questions from West German into the common Left German before I try to answer them. Furthermore, I shall, if I may, occasionally answer not the questions you asked, but those you ought to have.

(Whether changes in West Germany should be brought about within the framework of the West German constitution)

The worst thing about this constitution, as if it was not bad enough, is that it is about to get a lot worse. Though it is the constitution of what is essentially a cold dictatorship, it still includes certain republican freedoms. The big bourgeoisie is working very hard to get rid of it, which seems to me reason enough to defend it. Withdrawal of imperialist armaments, reduction of prices, rents and tariffs, a ban on the NPD (the neo-Nazi National Democratic Party) and legalisation of the KPD (Communist Party of Germany), protection of the most elementary of worker's rights – all such invigorating measures are provided for, even desired by, the current constitution. Perhaps it will one day come to pass that the fight to protect the constitution turns into a general demand for its democratic improvement. That wouldn't be so bad.

Question 2: How would you rate the chances of a new socialist or communist party in Germany?

Not great for a new communist party, pretty good for the old one.

Question 3: Would the extra-parliamentary opposition in Germany have to become anti-parliamentary or how could change in society be achieved otherwise if contemporary society is "incapable of any qualitative change in and of itself" (Rudi Dutschke)?

(Whether the extra-parliamentary opposition should become anti-parliamentary)

The principal purpose of the extra-parliamentary opposition must be the reinstitution of the parliamentary opposition, that is, the legalisation of the Communist Party. If it is true that the opposition is the heart of parliament, then such an implantation might well lead to a resuscitation of this dead body. I'd say that's rather important. In spite of itself, West German politics includes certain remnants of parliamentary traits. And given that the normal path toward a fascist dictatorship is significantly impeded by what are principally external circumstances (the existence of the GDR, the prevention of an immediate war of aggression by both Warsaw Pact and force de frappe[6]), it is not impossible that it will have to retain such parliamentary traits for some time yet, affording the Left multiple opportunities. The ruling class continually op-

6 French nuclear strike force.

erates with parliamentary and anti-parliamentary methods. Why shouldn't the opposition do the same?

Note: You will notice that questions 2 and 3 are misleading. They are so formulated as to make no provision for the right answer, roughly following the model: "Do you believe that giving frogs high-protein feed could help raise milk production?"

Question 4: In your opinion, what kind of situation would justify a revolution against the state?

(What situation would justify a revolution)

A revolutionary one. A revolution is justified by the possibility of its implementation. Marx states, "whoever attempts a revolution in a non-revolutionary situation is an idiot" (I'm quoting from memory, out of pure laziness, as is alas so often the case; but he did say it). The task posed by a non-revolutionary situation is not to implement the revolution but to create the conditions for it by way of organisation, spreading of class consciousness and the search for allies. It is not the same in politics as in the free arts. In politics, people are only clever when they are not clever alone.

Question 5: Do you think violence or a "just war" are legitimate means of carrying out a revolution against the existing system or do you envision other forms of confrontation?

(Whether violence is a possible means of revolution against the existing system)

Of course, but an unpleasant one. The purpose of a socialist revolution is the establishment of a free, just and peaceful world. All use of violence is principally absurd for the socialist revolution. The classical revolutions, the French and Russian revolutions, occurred without bloodshed. In both cases, the incorporation of bodily harm into the rules of the game was subsequently reserved for the counterrevolution.

This fact is all the more remarkable given that what you baptise as the "existing system" is an ongoing act of violence in and of itself: the disorder forcibly reproduced on a daily basis, the private ownership of the means of production maintained with state power.

It is no secret that Capitalism can conceive of no reason to limit the extent of its barbarism, other than in its own interests. The Federal Government, which with explicit reference to the comparability of the situations declares itself in agreement with the extermination of the Vietnamese people, thereby shows that it would take the same pleasure in agreeing to the extermination of the German nation, were there to be any danger, under any circumstance, of the latter escaping its control. A similar proposition was once put to the German people by Hitler. Imperialists always prefer a dead people to a democratic people.

In short, the "existing system" will use every means at its disposal in the class struggle, whether it be tricks, coercion, war or any other means. The means of revolution will have to bear in mind those of its opponents. One thing is clear, however: the revolution has no reason to be more violent than its opponents, and it never will be.

Question 6: Do you think Marx's thesis of a classless society as a desirable end state to history is still feasible? Or do you think a permanent revolution from below is desirable? And where do you see theoretical or concrete points of departure for this?

(Whether a classless society is a desirable end state to history or a permanent revolution from below is more desirable)

Curiously put. The GDR, in which exploiting classes are no longer to be found, nevertheless undergoes continuous change and this happens with a rarely known acceleration. Of course, a classless society is not an end state, but a sequence of states that contradict and further each other without being limited by any end. A classless society is only the beginning of human history after all. If you're referring to the historical movements of the GDR, I think they are as rational as possible, and if you're referring to the layabouts, I do not think they are the incarnation of the world spirit. Lenin's concept of permanent revolution, conceived as the transition from a bourgeois, anti-tsarist revolution to a proletarian one, has most recently been misused to suggest a so-called third revolution, one against the socialist state. This is obviously reactionary, and where it is not intended as reactionary, it is nonsense. As long as a revolution, such as the socialist one, is still far from bringing all of its latent productivity to bear, every revolution against it becomes a counterrevolution. The Kronstadt uprising[7], June 17th 1953[8], the Hungarian counter-October[9] and Mao's revolt of the naive[10] have all proved this.

Question 7: Do you believe in a "reprogrammed human being"[11] in a reformed and free society? How might conflicts be handled in this free society?

(Whether I believe in a new reprogrammed human being in a reformed and free society, and how he deals with his conflicts)

I can tell you, just as any citizen of my country could, how one expropriates the expropriators. I can tell you how one brings about the liberation of productive forces under socialism. What else do you want me to tell you? You're investigating such mysterious things with such mysterious words; I'm afraid I'm at a loss for anything more to say.

7 1921 uprising of Russian sailors in Kronstadt against the Bolshevik government.
8 Anti-government protests in East Berlin.
9 1956 anti-government uprising in Hungary.
10 Cultural Revolution in China (1966–1976).
11 The formulation appeared in a conversation of the German weekly *Der Spiegel* with the philosopher Herbert Marcuse in 1967.

How Are Things in Socialism's Public Offices? (Excerpt from "The German Alexandrine Metre – On 'Prexaspes'"[12])

[. . .] how are things in socialism's public offices? In fact, the role of socialist bureaucracy is very similar to that previously played by the bureaucracy under absolutism. It wore away at the remaining fortifications of capital, brought order during the period of post-revolutionary confusion and, to this day, it watches over society for any attempted return by its opponents. However, it does not want to acknowledge this role too openly.

Lenin only ever uttered the word bureaucracy with disgust, and it is clear from his writings that he believed the job of defending against rear blows could now be taken up by other groups, the masses for example. It might well be possible that Lenin succumbed to the delusion of unrealistic expectations in the matter. We admire Lenin as an unshakable realist, but perhaps of all the ways of engaging with the world, realism is the boldest, and perhaps only the hopeful can be bold.

What is alarming, however, is that Stalin, using the purest of Leninist phrases, declares the same revulsion for this class. Given that we do not quite want to follow Stalin on this topic, we would best amend that last conjecture about Lenin. After all, it is hardly unheard of that in statecraft one speaks least about the very thing one is most intent on doing. What is frowned upon, we can safely say, is at work. The civil servant has been notionally abolished because he is, in practice, once again particularly indispensable.

The danger of the ever-evolving tendency towards well-meaning but anarchical self-helpers in economic matters does not only reside in the peasant classes, as the early theorists had assumed. And it is also hardly greater in the artisanal and small business sec-

12 Prexaspes, play by Hacks which he describes as a civil servant's tragedy.

tor; socialism has, with varying degrees of success, taken all these concerns into account and, over the course of time, more or less eliminated them. One kind of tool owner, however, has been overlooked: those with a good head on their shoulders.

As long as socialist society has not created institutions that allow industrious and inventive human beings to fulfil themselves through activity and with public acknowledgement, such fettered productive forces will not cease to irritate. Counteraction by civil servants may not exactly be an elegant solution to this difficulty but one that, as things stand, cannot be replaced.

If Lenin decries the Bolshevik bureaucracy for having the signing of papers as its sole activity, we, on the other hand, have naturally made some progress since then. The sole and exclusive activity of our pen-pushers is to never sign a paper.

[. . .]

There is one characteristic of the civil servant that I have failed to mention: their tendency to backslide. As a class with a particular enthusiasm for continuity and consolidation, they are unfortunately inclined to ally themselves with the very regressive tendencies they had set out to prevent, as soon as their art is rendered obsolete by increasing progress. The bureaucracy, which is opposed to particularism, always ends up assuming the habits of petty tyrants. It is the only useful class that leaves no positive traces in the future. As soon as their day is out, they spread the purest, darkest night. It then becomes rather difficult to get rid of them and they end up decapitated on the very same chopping block on which they rendered their services to history. [. . .]

As far as I can tell, there hardly exists a class that would be of absolutely no value to humanity. World history is not kind to idlers. Just as with the faults of any other group of people, the faults of the civil service are the faults of its virtues. The faults, in other words, in the absence of which it could not carry out its activities. This is why all satire on civil servants is so stupid and why it always ends up in cabaret. Wherever the civil servant needs to be, he has to be what he is. [. . .]

Now, there also exists a rather half-baked knowledge about the public side of the world. It is, so one thinks and feels; simply lies. The petty bourgeoisie, excluded from all state affairs, separates the individual into a withdrawn being and a public facade. It overlooks the fact that there is equally a public being and a private facade. No American Indian, nobleman, sportsman, ticket inspector or trade unionist would think to regard his social rituals as inauthentic actions. Notably, the Church knows that God, who has to unfortunately pour his spirit into all too unequal pots, is much more concerned with the shape of the pot than with whether there is actually much of the spirit in it. Then again, authenticity in the domestic sphere is sometimes nothing better than mere self-indulgence.

The feudal man has his truth outside, the bourgeois man inside. The man of imperialism neither has any truth outside nor inside. In socialism, the public and the so-called human way of being are more or less balanced. Which of the two is the more believable, the more real must be taken on a case-by-case basis.

If ever a drama in continuous alexandrine verse were to be written, it would have been under Stalin. The goal of Socialism in one country would have been akin to state reason, if at the time, the lack of a good historical conscience had not prevented socialism from committing fully to its objective with all its consequences, aesthetic ones included. But the situation has changed. I have come to consider it essential to mix prose with the alexandrine, which, as far as I know, has been done for the first time since the banishment of Hanswurst[13].

I attach great value to regarding public and private attitudes on

13 Comic character in German theatre who disturbed the serious action with his jokes; banned from the stage by Enlightenment aesthetics in the first half of the 18th century.

an equal footing. We are presently in the process of discovering the individual to a yet unknown extent. It is precisely for this reason that we encourage him toward public thinking and feeling. In the developed individual, the concerns of the self and the concerns of humanity infuse one another with vitality; socialism is simply the world revolution and the dacha. Each is a means and an end to the other. In both places man can be true and in accord with his nature, in both hollow and insincere. [. . .]

The Latest from Biermann[14]

On 20.11.1976, the tabloid of the German bourgeois, known as *Der Spiegel*, granted an interview to the singing writer Wolf Biermann.

There is no need to introduce Biermann, he has done so himself. He was in Cologne where, with scientific terminology, rhymed songs and a great deal of winking and eye rolling, he suggested that achieving the goal of communism would be better served with bourgeois means.

As long as a workers' movement has existed, people like Biermann have been expelled from the party with the applause of history. Since Biermann said some very nasty things about the GDR and also alluded to the existence of a kind of club to implement these things, he has now been expelled from the GDR. The members of the said club apparently refer to each other as comrades, although one thing they certainly are not: members of a party so far known to be socialist.

He is now in West Germany, and I cannot say he has the look of a man who is unhappy there. Biermann got rather carried away. Indeed, he quite happily spilled his guts without the slightest of reservations. Not exactly the behaviour of someone in an environment he finds dispiriting.

For him to simultaneously claim, after all we had to hear from him, that he is concerned about the development of socialism in the GDR is about as credible as *Der Spiegel* publishing the same

14 Wolf Biermann, East German dissident who turned against the GDR government while at a concert in Cologne, West Germany, on November 13, 1976. On November 16, he was stripped of his GDR citizenship, which made it impossible for him to return. Numerous GDR artists protested against this decision, some of them publishing their criticism in Western media. Hacks' relatively late statement was directed not only against Biermann, but also against those of his colleagues who, in his eyes, were making pacts with the imperialist West.

stuff as always and adopting as its new title The Red Flag.

For any citizen of my country who might be curious to know how Biermann's been doing since then, I will tell you a little bit about the interview. It should be divided, if we go about this properly, into three parts.

In the first, Biermann says what he said in Cologne already. That he is no fan of the FRG and that he loves his country. He does not spare on declarations of intent, but they are a penny a dozen at the end of the day. "The Party Leadership" he claims, "must have been relieved after what happened in Cologne".

The second part looks at the tactical possibilities of Biermann's return to his old political workplace. The third is composed of your typical GDR-bashing and does not retain the investigative tone; Biermann uses poor justifications and uncouth language. He refers to the leadership of the SED as "Stalinist fat cats", which, leaving aside whatever you think or should think about Stalin, is obviously not an apposite description.

I would like to focus on the second part. Content-wise, it is the only one worth any attention. Biermann discusses with *Der Spiegel* how successful an application for GDR citizenship would be, though neither is in any doubt that such an application would be most unsavoury. "Who do you expect to help you?," the magazine asks.

Biermann has all sorts of suggestions.

1. He recommends that the SED should follow the examples of the Italian or French Communist Parties. Who am I to advise the SED? But I sincerely urge them not to do so. To heed Biermann's advice, they would have to establish an imperialist economy and regime in the GDR and enter into an insurrectionary relationship with it. To be frank, I'm quite happy that we have all that behind us, and I wish, if anything, that those powerful and ingenious fraternal parties will soon be as far along as we are. It is this and no other prescript that the philosophers of true socialism offer us in earnest.

2. He has got the approval of Heinrich Böll. Böll, as we all know, serves as the inn-keeper for dissident journeymen over there. Biermann spent the night in his bed, and I can only hope he did not find any of Solzhenitsyn's lice in it. I have seen Mr. Böll on television. He had eyes like one of those dogs in Thurber's cartoons and showed once again his practised astonishment at the fact that counterrevolution is prohibited in socialist countries.

3. He has, as *Der Spiegel* puts it, "his people in the GDR"; he has them wherever he goes apparently. Could the unification of the West German Left, asks *Der Spiegel*, be "a new challenge for you?"

Che Biermann (modestly) replies: "Perhaps a welcome side-effect." At times you really have to pity the man.

Both Biermann and his interviewers carefully avoid naming that list of GDR writers who have all declared they would like to have him back. Such caution is conspicuous; at the press conference the day before, Biermann had still put all his hopes in them. I would like to dwell a little on this particular point.

Informed, as I usually am, by the socialist press, I do not know the list referred to in its entirety. Indeed, I get far more frustrated with *Neues Deutschland* than with *Der Spiegel* because I read it more often. At a push, though, even with little news, you can figure out quite a lot, and any old hand could have more or less written the list down before it was even drawn up.

For the longest time, writers like ourselves have said much against each other. The subject of dispute is always the same: a writer's right to be uneducated. Quite a few believe that a writer should always make public whatever be his prevailing pensive ruminations. The others do not deny this for a moment, while not appreciating why this correct sentence should prevent an artist from occasionally taking a look at the first sections of "What is to be done".[15]

15 Lenin: *What Is To Be Done?* 1902.

Of course, the idea that the virtues of socialism could be combined with whatever meagre virtues imperialism still has to offer is undoubtedly pleasant. But the idea is, at the present moment, an uneducated one. It is the desire for a chocolate Leninism, and a Lenin made of chocolate would all too quickly melt away.

Writers demanding the right to be uneducated are obliged to be careful in regard to their subject matter. What the boy Biermann diddled away on his magic horn all those years ago, babbling on about whatever triviality happened to occur to him, was so very charming. Even then the rhymes were bad, the verses clumsy, and the ideas fuzzy. The words were too unimportant to go without music, and the melodies too weak to go without words. But Biermann's songs were as picturesque and whimsical as those sung by the shepherds in the fields or the chambermaids in the big cities.

It was not until he was driven by some misplaced ambition to draw himself up against Heine's philosophy and Villon's sense of the world, until he veered from everyday matters to those of the world, that he transgressed the genre appropriate to his talent and sank from folk singer to cabaret artist. He became what he is today; a variety show version of Eduard Bernstein.

Wolf Biermann is not as good as people think. It is not the first time I have pointed this out, and I would not be repeating this here if it didn't serve to explain him. Biermann bit off more than he could chew. And the more he did this, the more his art had need not just of guitars and poems, but scandals.

Biermann will not feel refuted by me (any more than any other artist to whom it applies). I quite approve of this intransigence. All artists have an eye for art and none an ear for reproaches. Artists are unaffected by any opinions, whether critical or political. The only thing that works on art is art. The only thing that can refute bad art is better art. But enough of all that and back to Biermann's Reconquista.

4. Namely and in conclusion, Biermann addresses the fear our state has of him. He tells *Der Spiegel* that the government of the

GDR was strong as long as it tolerated him. Now that it has gotten rid of him, however, it trembles. This assertion is meant to be its own proof; Biermann concludes the one from the other. I do not find it nearly as convincing as he does.

I have had a toothache since spring. I put up with the tooth because my dentist was having trouble with his liver or because I was travelling or some such reason. Now I intend to really have it removed and I can assure you it is no bigger pain now than it was in spring. I don't wish to claim, though certainly I could, that I was trembling before and now I'm strong. It just suits me to do it now.

Let us set aside the technical question of drawing the right conclusions for a moment. I think that by discussing his case in this context, Wolf Biermann is, perhaps, setting the threshold of fear in a socialist society a little too low.

One should not berate me unduly. Whatever conversations I had with Biermann were never particularly refreshing and without an intimate meeting of minds. Indeed, I'm happier speaking about him than with him. For reasons of fairness, I will give him the last word, and from the many good ones, I choose his most golden:

"Nothing happened in Cologne that would have tormented me in hindsight."

The Little Men With Their Ballheads

It is rarely easy to give a simple answer to a simple question. Recently, a pretty lady-friend of mine rather embarrassed me when she asked: Why, when there is the word revolutionary, why isn't there any evolutionary?

Well, I said, the run of things, you let them develop as they will. This is not an operation, there is no operator needed.

And, she says, if the run of things develops for the worse?

So, we need a word. Fortunately, the reformer comes to mind, which I offer to her. Then, all of a sudden, I am overcome with honesty and doubt. We have oldspeak and newspeak, oldthink and newthink; you need to be able to tell the difference. Many words, I explain, have naturally taken on a new meaning. Just take our neighbours to the West for example, who also speak some kind of German. For them, reform is just another word for deterioration. Reform of higher education, which means: less knowledge. Reform of healthcare, which means: less health. Reform of taxes, which means: more taxes. Our own word usage, I continue, is still in flux. Reform of socialism, for example . . . .

Gorbachev, my friend says, reminds me of Bahro somehow.

Absolutely, I say, Perestroika is the Russian word for New Age.

I mean, she says, these little men with their ballheads ...

The real controversial question in contemporary socialism is the extent to which the apparatus can be reformed. As far as civil servants go, we have a very impatient view of history. For example, we are quite used to seeing the hopes that absolutism could be reformed as wishful thinking, an illusion indeed. Yet the entirety of European civilisation, from the Renaissance to the classics, occurred during absolutism. If enlightened absolutism was an illusion, Michelangelo, Newton, Adam Smith, Goethe and Hegel all appeared within the conditions of this illusion.

Evolution, I said by way of conclusion, is the work of unravelling the possibilities inherent to a particular stage of history; work that demands a great deal of knowledge of reality as well as imagination.

My friend does not like to dwell on a particular topic. She changes the subject and enquires: Is there such a disease as brain rot?

If the prevailing symptoms are anything to go by, it would seem so.

She asks: Is it contagious?

Speaking of definitions: Lady-friends, pretty ones, in particular, are a bundle of charming expectations. But before I turn my attention to her, let me conclude what I was saying.

My friend is right of course. Those of us who call this place between the river Elbe and the Yellow Sea our home and for whom there are particular laws, other ones than those for the others – we need the evolutionary. We need the word and we need the person. The revolution created certain fundamental facts, and we have not yet put to use even one hundredth of their potential. The socialist revolution neither has to be made once again nor, for that matter, unmade. The October Revolution was not a disposable revolution.

Really, the evolutionaries of every socialist country should unite.

Letter to a Lady in Paris About a Place Called Germany

Dear Madam,

The best patriotism is one you never mention because it would never occur to you to do so. Were I to enquire as to your relationship with France, you too would be surprised and respond, "I'm French". Patriotism goes without saying, it is no different in the East.

What do I think of when I think of "Germany"? I'm a little taken aback and reply: Goethe and the GDR.

As was the case with the French nation, that of the GDR was brought about by revolution. Our concept of the state is most definitely Jacobin[16] and absolutely not that of Gironde.[17] The state and the nation coincide here. The idea of "reunifying" the GDR with the part leftover from the erstwhile German nation is sure to alienate every national instinct of a citizen of the GDR.

No doubt, some countries have relationships with certain others, which are more than simply businesslike. These relationships are more heartfelt. The distinction between domestic and foreign policy gets blurred: there are borders but they become, in a way, indistinct. For the GDR, such a country is the Soviet Union.

The Federal Republic of Germany is simply a neighbouring foreign country to the West. Communication is comparatively easy, because the people there speak German and because a number of them still remember Goethe and Hegel. But one can also speak quite enjoyably with French people who still remember Corneille and Voltaire, or with English people who have not forgotten Shakespeare and Adam Smith.

The social space of my aesthetic designs is the GDR. I am

16 Radical bourgeois wing that dominated the French Revolution during 1792–1794.

17 Moderate big bourgeois wing of the French Revolution.

easily bored: it has always bored me to write about imperialism, and I have never wasted a word on fascism. As subject material goes, they are stale and played out. I would feel provincial were I forced to make do with them.

Everybody has something to thank their fatherland for. Mine has spared me the effort of wasting time on questions that have already been answered. As a writer, I can thank the GDR for my being.

The Worst Socialism is Still Better Than the Best Capitalism (Excerpts from an Interview)

I never had any interest in abolishing socialism in the GDR, disagreed entirely with this enterprise, and have now quite visibly been proved correct, which does not help me any longer.

This land was unburdened of a bad socialism and was burdened instead with a bad capitalism, and every citizen of the country knows that it was a bum deal and would be happily rid of it.

What people struggle to understand is that even if the GDR had been made a normal constituent part of West Germany rather than a Generalgouvernement,[18] it would still have been a bum deal. In other words, people need to learn that the worst socialism is still better than the best capitalism. And they certainly are learning it. You teach them everything and then life achieves what forty years of Marxist school education did not. Two years of experience have done an awful lot. It's sad, that is as much as I can say about it.

Realistically speaking, I mean from the bottom of my heart, it would have been unthinkable for me to have done anything other than move to the GDR. The only alternative I can think of is death. What I did expect, though, here again, one comes uncomfortably close to the truth of things. I thought I would be entering a state of high Stalinism, but then I came after '53, June 17th [19] and the peculiar new direction things had taken then. It was a state of almost unbridled liberalism and every manner of freedom, which I rather enjoyed at the time, of course. It was even better than I had expected. The truth of it is, it was not at all that great, it was the first time the Soviet Union attempted to dump the GDR onto West Germany, a scheme they attempted several times, which finally

18 Administrative unit set up by Nazi Germany in its occupied territories in Poland.

19 See Fn 8 (A Revolution Against the State).

worked out now in '89. But they were trying it back then already. The liberalness was rotten and was all about foreign policy and wheeling and dealing.

The state did not fail, the state was abolished by an agreement between Moscow and Washington. There were two huge secret operations: The KGB, which controlled the better part of our State Security, on the one side, and the CIA, which owned a good part of the BND,[20] on the other. You can understand the KGB side a bit easier, given that it was formally in charge of State Security from the beginning. And it always had a wing that was simply a KGB wing with Markus Wolf as its main representative and it also had a wing that pursued a national GDR objective, so to speak.

20 Bundesnachrichtendienst (BND): foreign intelligence Service of the FRG.

The Task Before Us
The Restoration of a Revolution Cut Short

February was Bertolt Brecht's 100th birthday and the 150th of the Communist Manifesto. KONKRET, which otherwise has no great interest in such dates, spoke with Peter Hacks, who will soon be celebrating his own 70th birthday, about the meaning of these anniversaries and the relevance of the Manifesto.
konkret: Why do you think Brecht receives so much more applause than Marx and Engels?

Hacks: The honest old method of destroying reputations was to insult them to death. The question shows that, meanwhile, two more modern methods have been developed: death by silence and death by celebration. At present, they have chosen death by celebration for writers – this year, it was Brecht; last year, Heine; next year, Goethe. For Marx, it is death by silence. For their part, Brecht, Heine and Goethe were the victims of death by silence for years. In 1968, by contrast, it was Marx who was celebrated kaput by agents of the 4th International.[21] It is all the same in the end.

On television news programmes, one sees an awful lot of of spectres haunting Europe – from Kohl to Blair and from Václav Havel to Joschka Fischer. None of them bear any resemblance to communism. Have the "powers of old Europe," "Pope and Tsar, French Radicals and German police-spies", finally managed to bring communism to heel with their "holy witch-hunt"?

I never thought of the opening joke of the Manifesto as particularly felicitous. It is easy to remember, but it is not really clear what the metaphor is getting at. The idea, I suppose, is that com-

21 International political organisation founded in 1938 by Leon Trotsky in opposition to the Soviet Union and the Communist International (Comintern or the Third International).

munism is feared as though it were a spectre, though, in fact, it has flesh and blood and is alive and well. The men you mention, on the other hand, are actually spectres; nonetheless, I would advise everybody to be afraid of them.

Hunted down? Communism? No, how so?

The editor-in-chief of a left-wing weekly recently classified the "Communist Manifesto" as fiction, as you once did the bible in a letter to Kipphardt. "Of course, there is no claiming that the good Lord was right about everything, but he wrote a very good book." Does Hacks' designation also apply to Marx and Engels' pamphlet?

Marx and Engels wrote "a very good book", and in contrast to God, they were "right about everything". This they have in common with Hegel and Goethe. Even those who like praising the bible should admit that there has been progress in literature since then.

Around the time of the so-called turnaround, you wrote there is not "a fix that people could not make their way out of, most often battered, but never wiped out. There is no present, however miserable, without a future. Everything moves on, and as certain considerations and experience have shown, moves upward in the long run. Unless you get rid of the human race, with explosives, poison or mushrooms, it will see fit to move on and move up." In light of what is happening with the German working class, has your optimism suffered?

Permit me to say a word or two about the Manifesto, which is not called "The Communist Manifesto" incidentally but "The Manifesto of the Communist Party". The word party should not be neglected. The working class, the party and the socialist state, these are the three legs upon which the tripod of scientific-materialist Pythia[22] rests without wobbling.

22 Priestess at Delphi in ancient Greece, who announced her prophecies from a tripod (known as the Oracle of Delphi).

The program for the proletarian revolution appeared before the bourgeois revolution, which proved premature and never actually happened. In 1872 Engels seemed rather relieved that German capitalism slowly roused itself into corresponding, to some degree, to the picture that the authors of the Manifesto had painted of it. I can hardly call the Marxist concept of time empirical. The question "when?" is the question that one would do better not to ask Marx. Seldom do his sentences correspond to the moment in time when he issues them. In recompense, they are always right, now for example.

The task now is not that of a revolution with few preconditions, the task is much easier; the restoration of a revolution cut short, something for which history rarely needs any more than fifteen years.

Thanking you for offering your condolences to the "German working class," I shall answer quite practically. In 1953, only eight years after liberation, the single edition of the Manifesto in the GDR had a circulation of 850,000 copies. The book had another thirty-five years to appear. The Manifesto is also included in a number of selected or complete works, and even in the FRG a few hundred copies must have been printed. There are at least a million to be found on the shelves of the German working class, maybe two. The spirit of the working class has been institutionalised, and not weakly. I do not think the West German working class are as uneducated as they like to make out. They are perfectly aware of the stakes. I would rather refer to them as depraved or corrupted than stupid. The German bourgeoisie will yet regret having grafted onto their somewhat degenerated trunk the working class of the GDR, who were, I might add, not only well-read, but well-armed.

Does my optimism surprise you? I cast my lot, just as everybody else does, with the winning side. Capitalism doesn't have the slightest chance of survival.

The Names of the Left

NAKNAK THE ANT, ADAM, CONFUCIUS

Naknak the ant came to earth from the milky way, for it was a totem spirit and an authority on dreamtime. It wandered through a forest, teaming with all kinds of vermin, but Naknak could tell the difference between them and called them by their names. This noteworthy undertaking transpired in Tasmania.

As the second chapter of the story of creation tells us, the same work was carried out in our part of the world by Adam, the human. "For when the Lord God had made of the earth all manner of beasts of the field and all manner of birds of the air, He brought them unto man to see what he called them; for as man would call all manner of living creatures, so should they be called."

The general consensus since time immemorial is that it is not stupid to give things their due names. To give something a name is, in principle, no different to bringing it into being, or would you say that living creatures for which there is no more precise a word than "beasts and birds" actually exist? Earth-dwellers of old, named after nothing, were themselves nothing. They lived in a state of dereliction, free from reason or morals, it was nothing but promiscuity and a Gomorrah.

Of the teachings of Confucius, the most famous is quite rightly: "Were the Emperor to ask you to administer the government, what would you do first?

The master replied: Rectify the names without fail" (Lun Yu[23] X III-3). It seems to me that one group in no less need of correction today than beasts and birds in the past is the members of the political left. Below, I will attempt to make them comprehensible and put them in order.

23 Lun Yu (Analects of Confucius), one of four texts of the teachings of Confucius.

NATURAL SYSTEM OF THE LEFT

1. Communists. Marxist-Leninists who have made it their goal to promote the replacement of the monopoly capitalist social formation by a socialist social formation. Parties: CPSU until 1953. SED until 1971. KPD. Also: All-Union Communist Party Bolsheviks.

2. Reform communists. The moral collapse of the CPSU occurred after the victory over Hitler as suddenly as a crisis after the peak of an economic boom. Things took a definitive turn on the day the party learned that rather than dedicating themselves to glory, peace and reconstruction, they would have to invent the atomic bomb. Stalin had once before solved the problem of making up a backlog of one hundred years in ten and paid for it with the most terrible economic sacrifices and the most horrific of all wars. The Soviet communists also embarked on this task, but in their weary minds they were plagued by the thought of whether there might not be a way of avoiding the next war. It is not a matter of our understanding how fed up they were. It was a pointless thought that led to a pointless hope and the hope to opportunism. After Stalin's death, the international workers movement gives up and splits into left and right deviations. Both left and right deviations declare themselves adherents of the pure doctrine and expel one another out of the international workers movement. The schism takes up the second half of the 20th century. Reform communists are those right-wing opportunists who believe that the questions of both peace and socialism can be entrusted to the able hands of imperialism ("historical compromise"). Theories derived from Hilferding, Kautsky, Otto Reinhold. Rejection of Stalin. Parties: CPSU (Khrushchevites/Brezhnevites), also: Eurocommunists. The DKP was collectively founded by L. Brezhnev, Willy Brandt and Luigi Longo in 1968 against the opposition of Max Reimann and Walter Ulbricht.

3. Maoists. Left-wing partners in the opportunistic schism.

Believe that honest courage alone can offset economic facts. Parties: KPD/ML.

4. Independent social democrats. Derivative of the pre-revisionist Bebel tradition of the SPD from 1917 to 1922. A transitional phenomenon and theoretical hybrid that disintegrated into the SPD and KPD. Party: USPD.

5. Communist Platform, namely of the PDS. This swindle, founded in 1990 by three agents of the counter-revolution, Lothar Hertzfeld, Fred Beuchel and Marian Krüger, nevertheless managed to work its way up to the level of a USPD, which ought in the first place to have been called UPDS.

6. Socialists. All socialist parties are of the same nature and origin as the USPD, they just last longer. The classic model is Mussolini's and Nenni's PSI.

7. Bourgeois left. No interest in Marx and Lenin, but credible antimilitarists and antifascists. Critique of imperialism in the tradition of John A. Hobson. Party: German Peace Union (DFU).

8. National left. Sporadic phenomenon in young nation states. Critique of imperialism in the tradition of the Mahdi. Kemalists, Peronists, Nasserites. Parties: Baath.

9. Radicals. Strong petty-bourgeois current in France following in Voltaire's footsteps, corresponding to the German Free-Minded Party. According to Lenin, they should be excluded from the revolution. Party: Republican, Radical and Radical-Socialist Party of France.

10. Trotskyites. Communists whose principal goal is the opposition of Stalin. Parties: SAP, KAPD.

11. Anarchists. Supporters of Bakunin and Kropotkin, opponents of Marx.

12. New Left. Conceived by Herbert Marcuse for the CIA, lively ephemeral influence after the first post-war crisis in the sixties and the need for accumulation following the technical revolution. To be categorised, like numbers 10 and 11, as part of the groupings of the 4th International. Party: Student movement.

13. Terrorists. Nechayevist comrades who cause and suffer indescribable and quite unnecessary trouble. Parties: RAF, 2nd September movement.

14. Majority socialists. The remains of social democracy after the USPD quit. No left-leaning tendencies. The current chairman, Gerhard Schröder, belongs either to the right wing of the FDP or directly in Brussels. Curiously, the term majority socialist has the same meaning as the word Bolshevik. Parties: SPD, PDS.

15. Individual communists. Communists with a flaw or a 'Puschel' (A 'Puschel' in theatre language: characteristic trademark). Hermann L. Gremliza, for example, a Germanophobe and a philosemite but, in all other respects, a communist. Similarly, Georg Fülberth, Holger Becker, Gerhard Branstner. Often astute, but just every man "in his humour". Unsuitable for parties.

CALL TO ORDER

The reason for the dissatisfaction and irritation of many leftists is that instead of sitting together amiably in their respective hangouts, some strange fate has seen fit to sort them into other places. Their names are wrong. They do not fill the bill of where they are.

Why are Kurt Gossweiler and André Brie members of one and the same party when neither of them belongs there? What are Hans Heinz Holz and Ellen Weber doing in one and the same party, when neither of them belongs there? Why didn't Rolf Vellay ever become a member of the party he always wanted to be in? I expect my proposal of a Natural System to have more than a trivial effect on all those concerned.

After Adam had told the deer that it was a deer and the goat a goat, the deer finally stopped fucking the goat.

Georg Nostradamus or the Predictions of Professor Fülberth[24]

500 YEARS OF IMPERIALISM

Georg Fülberth has made a discovery of decisive importance to every inhabitant of the globe. The imperialist mode of production, as he has discovered, will continue for another 500 years.

The proof is as follows. Slave society lasted from 500 years before to 500 years after Christ, so 1000 years. Feudalism lasted from the year 500 to 1500, that is again 1000 years. Capitalism, which began in the year 1500, thus has another 500 years to rake in the full 1000 years to which it is duly entitled.

Every mode of production, as the list shows, is entitled to 1000 years. I would have taken Fülberth's millennium magic for a joke had his title "Short Leaps" (*konkret* 4/2000) not led me to suspect that he attaches a certain importance to this doctrine of his on the long-windedness of social formations. Moreover, Manfred Sohn (in nVs 1/2000[25]) had already unveiled his general "reflections on the dimension of time in politics" three months before Fülberth (We Marxists, Sohn chides us, are always "excessively hasty" and our conclusions are all "premature").

When I realised that Fülberth's calculation was meant seriously, I decided to make some calculations of my own. I arrived at the following historical account, which I believe to be closer to the truth.

24 This article is Hacks' rejoinder to an article by Georg Fülberth – "Short Leaps" – published in the left-wing German monthly magazine *konkret*, 4/2000 (pp. 36–37), in which Fülberth argued that imperialism was stable and would last for a long time. The rejoinder, which appeared in *konkret* 10/2000 (pp. 42–46), also discusses the theories of imperialism of Hilferding, Luxemburg and Lenin, among others.

25 Neue Volksstimme (new voice of the people)

I put Asiatic despotism (China, Egypt, Mesopotamia) at 3000 or 4000 years.

Just as Fülberth did, I give the slave owners 1000 years, from 500 before to 500 after.

Feudalism I give the years 800 to 1500, so 700 years (The missing 300 years from 500 to 800, which are neither slave-owning nor feudal in nature, I give to Robert Kurz, I'm not interested in them. They could be said to have something of this neither-capitalism-nor-socialism diagnosis, which he applies to the present moment of all things. I'm sure he'll like them).

Following this, according to my calculations, from 1500 to 1900, 400 years of absolutism, including Bonapartism (This is that period of bourgeois-feudal compromise; indeed the only period during which freely competing capitalists were allowed to share a bit of power and go about their business).

Imperialism gets 100 years, from 1900 to 2000, and its time is basically up.

That is what I wanted to prove.

You will have recognised, thanks to the intelligence tests you've passed in the course of your life, that each period is 300 years shorter than the one that preceded it. We are dealing with the type of series of decreasing arithmetic progressions as a general law of historical periods. After imperialism, we should prepare for another 3000 to 4000 years of socialism. To say any more on the subject would be reckless and no longer strictly scientific.

WHAT A COMMUNIST WOULD HAVE ASKED

Great discoverers are boastful, I'm not reproaching Georg Fülberth for that. But the prognosis of 500 years of imperialism and declarations such as: "Capitalism is currently simply bursting with strength" – what use are such lessons to the working class? Couldn't it be that such lessons dampen their spirits? A communist would have considered that question. Fülberth reveals his terrible secret for all to hear, blurting out to all peoples and classes quite brutally and unsparingly that the powers that torture us are not set to collapse for another half a millennium.

Every day, one sees imperialism crumbling, but one would, of course, still like to be courteous with Georg Fülberth. Personally, I have every reason to thank him. He corrects my mistakes in Latin. He comes to my defence when a hostile party organ attempts to annihilate me. He reviews my poems with great warmth. I have found a way of giving Fülberth his due and can acknowledge this much: imperialism is unlikely to die at the hands of Georg Fülberth.

A communist would have also considered the following question: What has Marxism had to say about the historical outlook for imperialism up to now? The communist is, as we know, dogmatic, a slave to authority and someone who takes the written word as gospel. But he may be somewhat excused by the fact that his opponents are usually seriously lacking in arguments against Marxism. Indeed, it is extremely rare that they dispute something Marxists have actually thought or said. They would much rather disprove Marxist theories that no Marxist has ever proposed.

"Marxist science," according to Fülberth, predicted "the end of imperialism." That's it, and nothing more. But with that he attributes a notion to the entire pre-Fülberthian Marxist tradition that no classical Marxist was ever inclined to entertain. He thus leaves me no choice but to relieve him of this burden he has taken on – that of reporting on the assumptions of Marxist authorities regarding the time and manner of the death of imperialism.

THE END OF IMPERIALISM ACCORDING TO THE SCIENCE OF MARXISM

1. Karl Marx. *Capital I, 1867. Historical tendency of capital accumulation.* Marx, who died before imperialism was born, formulated the complete theory of imperialism with an assortment of memorable observations. "One capitalist always kills many,"

"centralisation of capital," "the monopoly of capital becomes a fetter upon the mode of production,", "socialisation of labour bursts asunder," the private "capitalist integument," "the knell sounds," "the expropriators are expropriated." The conclusion of these ingenious formulations promises the exploiter no particular Doom of the Gods beyond the fact that somebody will eventually come and relieve him of what he has taken.

The genius of Marx was his art of solving problems before they had appeared. As far as judging existing problems goes, Napoleon I, Goethe, Hegel, Lassalle and Napoleon III were a lot more worldly-wise and realistic, not to mention Lionel Rothschild.

2. John A. Hobson. *Imperialism*, 1902. The man who Fülberth quotes so respectfully is called Hobsbawm and is somebody else. Among all the commentators on imperialism, Hobson is the only one who, as a late Victorian Englishman, actually knows what he's talking about. He compares the decline and fall of imperialism with the decline and fall of the Roman empire and issues the former a sort of oracle-like threat, a type of curse: "The laws which, operative throughout nature, doom the parasite to atrophy, decay, and final extinction. Its penalty is unalterable in the order of nature".

I can say neither from the context nor the formulation if "extinction" means "dying out" or "death through external influence." Whether it was "extinction" or "extinguishment" that Hobson used in the original, both terms are ambiguous.

I maintain: Imperialism will die, or it will be made to die.

3. Rudolf Hilferding. *Finance Capital*, 1905. Somewhat better known for the rather entertaining thought: "Today, taking possession of six large Berlin banks would mean taking possession of the most important spheres of large-scale industry." The analyst of promoter's profit has quite unequivocal ideas about "the ultimate phase of the class struggle" and the "conquest of political power".

The idea of an economic collapse "makes no sense". Rather: "In the violent clash of these hostile interests, the dictatorship of the magnates of capital will finally be transformed into the dictatorship of the proletariat."

4. Rosa Luxemburg. *The Accumulation of Capital*, 1913, as well as *An Anti-Critique*. Imperialism, more so even than capitalism, suffers from crises caused by a lack of appropriate demand. Accumulation is thus only possible through the additional exploitation of non-capitalist "other consumers," so-called "third persons". That is, small producers who help domestic and foreign monopolies to gain access to their markets. Imperialism, once it has absorbed all third persons and divided them up among itself, is left together with its waged proletariat as "pure imperialism": just Krupp and Krause. In this hour of its absolute victory, it ultimately croaks from overproduction. Krupp and Krause have divided the value of Krause's work among themselves, and should Krupp find no buyer other than himself, Krupp, and his employee, Krause, then Krupp's reproductive capacities are limited to that of his own capital, and so he has to reach for his gun.

I can empathize with Luxemburg's satisfaction at having been able to hurl this theory into the world in two robust volumes.

What she added to the knowledge of the world is nothing less than a mathematical concept for what is observable. The evident outrages that imperialism engenders are the expropriation of peasant land and the hunting down of negroes, and Rosa's economic and moral world formula shows that insofar as imperialism wipes out peasants and negroes, it wipes out those who sustain it. Thus, by these very circumstances, as in melodrama, its descent into hell results directly from its own sins.

Luxemburg's intellectual edifice (also stolen from the Narodniks) is somewhat correct and, in the main, erroneous. It is to her credit to have brought "third persons" and "pure imperialism" to the table, from whence they cannot now be removed. We encounter third persons under the new name of civil society, but in their old role as avengers, in the works of Gramsci and subcomandante Marcos. As regards pure imperialism, of whose fictitious nature nobody can be in doubt, Schröder's government is trying to summon it into the realm of actual facts right before our astonished eyes.

Not to slander a great woman. Although Luxemburg states that imperialism will perish of its own accord, she urgently advises that we beat it to death beforehand.

5. Vladimir Ilych Lenin. *Imperialism, the Highest Stage of Capitalism*, 1916. Quoting Hobson and Hilferding freely, Lenin's classic leaves very little room for improvement. As the author himself explains, the book was written "with an eye to the tsarist censorship" and "in a slavish tongue", which is why it gives less space to the economic or political demise of imperialism. Towards the end of the text, Lenin expands his definition of imperialism to include one further feature; that of "moribund capitalism", which, as Lenin so pointedly remarks, will have to "inevitably be removed".

In the language of a free man, with no regard for tsarist censorship, Lenin shares his opinions on the disappearance of imperialism in *Prophetic Words*, 2.7.1918. I'd rather you read it, but I will give an idea of what it says.

Lenin refers to Engels, who in 1887 wrote that after the next world war, "the victory of the proletariat will either be already achieved or at any rate (*doch*) inevitable". Lenin links this to the question of what consequences might be deduced from the ongoing civil war, "without which not a single serious Marxist has conceived the transition from capitalism to socialism."

6. Nikolai Bukharin. Knows that "pure imperialism" is not possible and that there is never any shortage of "third persons." He hurls at Luxemburg's two volumes two of his own: *Economics of the Transformation Period*, 1922 and *Imperialism and the Accumulation of Capital*, 1926.

I'll leave it at that, particularly as Bukharin shares with his opponent a certain penchant for being difficult to use.

There are some concluding remarks of Stalin's to be added to Bukharin's critique of Luxemburg. Incidentally, Stalin would like it to be understood that he is the originator of points 7, 8 and 9.

7. *History of the Communist Party of the Soviet Union (B)*, with the publication deadline set by the Central Committee under Stalin for 1938, just as the Bible had its canon closed by the great synod under Ezra at the end of the 2nd century. The history book takes up Lenin's concept of "moribund capitalism" and summarizes his theory of imperialism as follows. "This, of course, did not mean that capitalism would die away of itself, without a revolution of the proletariat, that it would just rot on the stalk. Lenin always taught that without a revolution of the working class, capitalism cannot be overthrown."

8. Eugen Varga. *Basic Questions of the Economics and Politics of Imperialism after the Second World War*, 1953. This scholar detects a "period of general crisis of capitalism" and declares: "the stage of prosperity is excluded from the cycle." Indignant that "after the second world war" both the Americans and the social democrats succeeded in cheating the Soviet Union of the fruits of victory, he consoles himself with the third one: "inevitable defeat will put an end to the whole system of imperialism."

9. The Academy of Sciences of the Soviet Union (Institute for Economics) delights us with its brilliant *Political Economy*, Textbook, 1954.

"Capitalism", according to the book, "is fully ripe for replacement by ... socialism". It is dying

- from past and present socialist revolutions,
- from its imperialist wars,
- from the liberation movements of the colonised peoples.

"This does not mean", the textbook summarises sensibly, "that capitalism can die by itself, through "automatic collapse" without resolute struggle by the masses of the people, headed by the working class."

So that we are all quite clear on the matter: The more sick and feeble you are, the easier the job of Godfather Death.

10. Otto Reinhold. *Imperialismus heute* (Imperialism today),

1965. The Khrushchevite conspiracy, with its convergence of imperialism and socialism, including the peaceful resolution of all contradictions, first came to light in the GDR in the above-mentioned fundamental work, before its recent reappearance in G. Fülberth's writings. Alongside Reinhold, Heinz Petrak also has to be mentioned here.

I shall report by quoting.

Reinhold says of imperialism that through it "a conscious exploitation of the economic laws of capitalism occurs, under the direction of the monopolies, and with the help of the regulatory activity of the state." "There are still many people today", he claims, "who expect a swift surge in class struggle basically only after another economic crisis erupts." Such a view is, however, both "erroneous and demobilising."

The view of Reinhold himself is not demobilising. "The more the working class succeeds in limiting monopoly power in West Germany and gaining influence over its regulatory mechanisms, the better it is placed to fight for a larger share of these vast riches even under conditions of capitalism." Anybody who doubts this has an "erroneous and dogmatic view of capitalism."

11. Walter Ulbricht. *100 Years of "Capital"*, 1967.[26] His rebuttal of Reinhold was not long in coming. On convergence: "The essence of state monopoly capitalism as a social order, as a whole, is naturally diametrically opposed to socialism." *On the 150th birthday of Karl Marx*, 1968. On the non-antagonistic, evolutionary, and, as it were, seamless transition from imperialism to socialism: "The doctrines of the various bourgeois and social-democratic ideologues aim to give you the impression that the cycle of crisis, depression, boom and war can be overcome by virtue of faith-healing or by the pure power of persuasion."

Before he was liquidated by the Russians, Walter Ulbricht left his testament in his last speech. "The unity and cohesion of the in-

26 Reference to the paper presented by Ulbricht at the International Scientific Session: 100 Years of Capital – Berlin, 12./13. Sept 1967.

ternational communist movement" must "be forged at higher levels".

12. Sahra Wagenknecht. *Kapital, Crash, Krise* (Capital, Crash, Crisis) 1998. Expands on Hilferding in considering the technical and quantitative innovations on the markets of fictitious capital in the last one hundred years. The "end of culture", which Luxemburg declares as the sorry plight of a declining imperialism that has escaped socialism, has for Wagenknecht a hint of fascism to it. I cannot, for the life of me, see why fascism would be a source of sorrow for imperialism. Fascism, along with neoliberalism, is, after all, one of the forms in which the imperialist state, since its genesis, has waited on the monopolies that are its master. Fascism was more suitable for depressions, neoliberalism for the boom periods. Both are good, however, and can be employed at will and, if need be, even simultaneously.

The philosopher formulates her hopes for the impermanence of imperialism by declaring: "I am sure that in the long run, people will not stand for what capitalism does to, and with, them. They will defend themselves and look for alternatives, which can only be found beyond the prevailing economic system."

Wagenknecht says what Lenin says, but I have to admit I find Lenin's slavish language somehow handier than Wagenknecht's slavish language.

THE UNANIMOUS JUDGMENT OF MARXISTS

If we impute to Luxemburg a certain left-wing zeal and disregard Otto Reinhold as a non-Marxist, the Marxist maxim on the fate of imperialism is: It won't go down without a kicking. A good kicking and down it'll go.

Of course, nobody can stop imperialism from slipping on a banana skin and breaking its neck. On the other hand, as long as the leaders of the world's proletariat here go by the names of Gysi, Stehr, Baier, Hue or D'Alema, imperialism can damn half the workers to unemployment, damn half the unemployed to homelessness and sleep as carefree as a kitten while doing so.

Nobody can put a date on the unavoidable demise of imperialism. Marxists have learned to keep quiet on the topic of dates. Fülberth is very much on his own when he takes the liberty of declaring that it will take a very, very long time yet.

IMPERIALISM IS INTOLERABLE

Georg Fülberth wants to know whether I think an end to imperialism "as soon as possible" is desirable. I am suitably flattered; apart from him, barely anybody has ever considered my opinion to be of the least importance. What it comes down to, however, is whether the planet finds imperialism tolerable. People don't revolt until something has become intolerable.

There are, in fact, a number of depredations caused by imperialism that could well render it intolerable, I count three.

The first occurred to Fülberth already. It is the so-called, dramatic "big crash", coined by August Bebel, and renamed by Fülberth as the definitively dramatic "final crash". He is referring to the global economic crisis, known in scientific language as a "general" or "universal" crisis. Otto Reinhold presumes, and Fülberth presumes with him, that depression has forever been regulated out of existence from modern imperialism's crisis cycle.

Stalin, however, if we recall, decreed that it was the boom that had disappeared from the crisis cycle. There is something to be said for each of these views. It is certainly true that the course of crises has continued as a whole but in a more indistinct form. The rule does not apply with any regularity. It occurs more flatly, but more often, and both the phases and the periods in between are less pronounced and tend to overlap. If the crisis cycle were a menstrual cycle, they'd say imperialism was suffering from spotting and needs to see an oncologist.

The fact that someone has cancer doesn't really make him any easier to manage.

The palace of the global economy is a speculative building of bad credit and unsecured money. Everything about its fall is probable and nothing improbable. Wasn't it only in 1999 that the crisis engulfed East Asia, Russia and South America? For the great crash itself, only the USA and Europe were missing, and not by much.

The other evil is world war.

"In the meantime", says Fülberth, meaning since the general despondency after the second world war, "wars may once again be wageable" – and with "may" he means simply "are". With wageable, he means winnable by America or German Europe.

The sentence can be understood in two different ways. Firstly: Wars may once again be waged, then it was right this once, namely in regard to the war against Iraq; those times have already passed now. Secondly: Wars can once again be waged. This is how Fülberth himself understands it, in which case it is simply untrue.

I cannot help but wonder how the writer can skip over, carelessly, amused even, the damage that war causes imperialism. As if wars were imperialism's favourite state of affairs. For some idiotic reason, he behaves as though the twentieth century had belonged to imperialism and as though it had had, thanks to its Protean nature, an easy-going and unchallenged life behind it.

The truth is: After World War I, imperialism had lost control of over a sixth of the earth. After World War II it retained half at most. Were it not for one imperialist country among all others, one which akin to England in the olden days, lives on an island and scrupulously avoids making a personal appearance in any of the wars for which it pays – were it not for the USA, both wars could well have meant the end for imperialism.

A number of outcomes of both world wars were lost for socialism thanks to the USA. Or maybe not. One shouldn't make oneself out to be even more stupid than one actually is, and one should stop speaking of the luminaries of actually existing socialism as though of a society of losers.

The game, incidentally, which imperialism won against socialism at the end of the century was not a war. This may be grounds for celebration or grounds for alarm, but we have not lost a war to date. Not one.

An explanation for this can be found, by anyone looking for it, in Karl Kautsky's pretty fascicle *Der Bolschewismus in der Sackgasse* (Bolshevism at a Deadlock): "Bolshevism was from the very beginning a conspiracy after the Blanquist model, built up on the blind obedience of the members towards their autocratic leaders. In this point Bolshevism and militarism meet. All its successes, therefore, are in spheres where military methods can be applied."

If I were Fülberth, I would reconsider just how feasible the waging of imperialist wars actually is.

The third way in which imperialism is in choppy waters, is the "economic law that the relations of production must necessarily conform with the character of the productive forces" (Stalin, *Economic Problems of Socialism in the USSR*). In other words, the law of the absolute ineptitude of the capitalist mode of production for the newer forces of production. Imperialism is dying from the fact that it has reached its limits and is destroying pretty much everything.

Permit me, if you will, to dwell on the obvious and superficial. The social form of imperialism, which was once a revolution and accelerated the productive forces more than any system of production before it, has been choking on its own contradictions for the last hundred years of its existence.

It seems particularly strange to consider how much future imperialism has, given that it has long been undeserving of a present. Never has there been a social system, whose uselessness was so patently written across its forehead. What am I talking about? Well,

- its railways, thundering into motorway bridges,
- its transatlantic aeroplanes, falling from the skies and next to the runways,
- its cars, cruising out of the factory gates and right into the repair shops.

Its Mars rovers do not reach Mars. Its telegrams take longer than the post. Its renowned newspapers are no longer ashamed of misprints. There is no meat in its sausages and no raspberries in its jam. The food is so bad that you can quite reasonably say that the German middle class has nothing to eat.

The outrageous sums of money shelled out by the imperialist state to its monopolies in the form of tax breaks and direct subsidies prevent any solvent demand. Three per cent growth is considered a boom, with the service industry included. If they cannot sell something, it never occurs to them to improve it or make it cheaper. Instead, they go on a publicity campaign.

What rays of hope for the future does Fülberth open up for imperialism, given the inevitable crises, the inevitable wars and the inevitable failure of its mode of producing commodities?

Without wanting to push him too far in the direction of the court astrologer of Charles IX, Fülberth's two arguments in favour of another half-millennium of imperialism are rather thin. He appears to believe in a future of free heart operations for insolvent geriatrics. He also appears to believe, if I understand him correctly, in a future of efficient "regulation of the financial markets" – that is pretty much it. Not an iota of it is worth refuting.

I, who have lived my life under socialism and know it as well as Hobson knew his imperialism, assure Fülberth: producing all these world-spanning and long-lasting things, but also distributing them calmly and coolly, only we can do that.

POSTSCRIPT

This riposte of mine has come rather late. I must apologise to Georg Fülberth and also to the *konkret* editors, I really have dawdled. If I manage to still make it on time before imperialism collapses, then everything will have worked out fine. If imperialism kicks the bucket before this essay against it is published, well it will be my own fault and my own tough luck.

Dispute at the Wailing Wall

Vellay: Imperialism modernises production, after which, we take control of it.

Hacks (agrees).

My agreement, dear Vellay, is limited to certain considerations, such as, for example, the following.

We already took production away from imperialism in 1917 and 1946, which was far from foolish.

It greatly improved the level of civilization in both Russia and China for example. East Germans were also much better raised and a lot less daft than those in the West.

In East German Socialism, there were edible bread rolls and edible bread, you can read Ulbricht's theory on it ("We should not imitate the infantile disorders of imperialism"). I would prefer not to eat Mr. Kamps' bread rolls.[27]

Low prices at Aldi and Walmart and low telephone charges serve to set the high prices and charges that you and I will have to cough up once the final pecking order of the monopolies has been established.

Job cuts are not much use to those who have been cut, given that neither companies nor banks are particularly likely to continue paying them or indeed to engage them in any other useful activity. Only socialism can survive without a reserve army.

Who will buy the capitalist's commodities once all the non-capitalists have gone bankrupt?

Plenty of people I know do not like to wage war.

In a nutshell, imperialism already wastes and worsens productivity to at least the same extent as it is a motor of such. If we refrain from complaining about that, how on earth are we supposed to keep the party entertained before it decides to lead the masses?

27 Kamps is the largest German bakery chain, which delivers industrially prefabricated dough for baking to its branches.

In the End They Even Understand It (Excerpt from an Interview)

Imperialism has decided to opt for barbarism, rather than socialism. This is the most essential aspect of the present era. As it turns out, everybody is unhappy. Curiously enough, the human being as a species is not particularly fond of barbarism. The grand new myths that have appeared, the politically ill-founded but huge popular movements, give me hope that you can do almost anything to people, but not absolutely everything. In a hundred years, something might well come of it. But one cannot write a play about that.

There is another line from "Die Maßgaben der Kunst" (The Stipulations of Art)[28]: "Every day, one sees imperialism crumbling." The next war has been slated. . .

Imperialism is bound to fall apart, it is already doing so. Presently, you can see the American bloc battling against the European bloc. What the Asian bloc looks like we do not yet know, it has still to be constituted, but it has at least already dared to stand up to America. The situation with these three blocs is quite clear and will lead to war.

So, a war motivated by weakness?

No, by the distribution of what little money there is. Imperialism has murdered all its clients and is surprised why nobody is buying any of its wares. So now they have to wage war over the few people left to buy anything.

Back then, during the war, it mattered when you asked: "Who is the baddie?" If Bush has Hitler's role today, then things don't look good for him at present. The fact that he has the baddie's role

28 Collection of essays by Hacks.

and everybody knows it, will make things difficult for him. This is why he might not win now, or it will be a Pyrrhic victory, which will not go down well with him.

You describe the era of decline as beginning with Ulbricht's departure from politics.

Everybody, apart from those at the junge Welt[29], knows that the decline started with Stalin's death. And the slow process of public affairs I described took from 1953 to 1973 to reach its conclusion. The final death blow came with the Ulbricht-murder enacted by Honecker and Brezhnev, something that cut into my heart and from which I have never recovered. From then on things began to go downhill. The world-historical context was the Helsinki Conference and the SED/SPD paper, that is, the social-democratisation of world communism. At that point, it was quite clear: There was no more saving it.

A movement that abolished itself?

Yes. Yes.

What do you think were the necessary preconditions?

When I asked my Russian translator what in the world did Gorbachev want, she gave me the only rational explanation I have ever heard: He belongs to the Azerbaijani drug mafia, and they need a convertible rouble. That really made me laugh, I thought it was very witty.

But I do not know anyone who could have paid Khrushchev. And I do not see why he needed a convertible rouble. It is for me a riddle wrapped in a mystery inside an enigma. At the time of Stalin's death, Russia was not doing badly. He had largely taken care of what problems the country had had. And socialism is, just like imperialism, a society that can crawl its way out of a crisis in

29 Marxist German daily that continually draws attention to Hacks' work.

surprisingly good shape and surprisingly quickly. First class people are not always replaced by idiots. Now and again idiots are also replaced by first class people. And although it may be mortifying for Marxists to admit, the person out front plays more than just a supporting role.

Which brings us back to the monarchy.

The advantage the monarchy has over socialism is that it is hard to get rid of. It is true that during absolutist times, the country flourishes if the prince is a great man but starves and loses wars if he is an idiot. But for the survival of the monarchy, the prince's talents have only seldom been decisive in world history. And even when you guillotine Charles of England or Louis of France, the people know that something new is coming, but then we'll need a king again. Socialism is, to start with, a scientific and conscious act of volition, and as such it can be revoked. And it has the innate capacity to give birth to counter-revolutionary souls. Whereby you bring me to a question that I have never stopped asking myself.

How could anybody ever think that this idea of peaceful co-existence would work?

I said as much at the time, in good faith we are placing the question of peace in the hands of imperialism. After that, there was nothing else to say. But the real mystery is that both the Politburos, in the Soviet Union and in the GDR, were well aware at all times that the West intended to abolish them with its peace. They were always telling each other: Watch out, the enemy has it in for us. Then they always acted as if the enemy did not have it in for us. Meaning, they abolished themselves, even though they knew they were abolishing themselves. [...]

If China becomes a capitalist country, there will be no Cuba left to talk of after Castro's death. Institutionalised communism, as a global movement, would indeed be wiped out. And all those dissatisfied people, the Bambulas[30] and the South American Presidents will be wondering how to make progress and make the revolution. And somebody will tell them, there are books about it. A cultural upsurge can sometimes be brought about in an incredibly short time. To that extent, I would say, even if I assume that the demise will persist in the short term, I also count on a revival, and one that is certainly not centuries away. The reason for the current crisis of imperialism is that it is bankrupt. This will undoubtedly grow into a global economic crisis. Everyone knows that global economic crises beget communist parties. And these communist parties have not been influenced in the least by the political demise of communism. They think as they have always thought, first unskilfully, then skilfully. In the end, they even understand it.

And when the global economic crisis and a meaningless war or a tendency to wars coincide, soon enough, you will have communist movements once again.

In other words: when something has been envisaged by the world spirit, you know you can rely on it.

World spirit? We'd certainly like a definition of that.

Then let me change the sentence. Anything I've once said, you can count on it.

30 Probably used here in the sense of drumbeaters or protestors.

On Art and Aesthetics

Literature in the Age of Science (Excerpt)

[. . .] Let's take the atom bomb as an example. Certain people claim they are obliged to write differently in the age of the atom bomb as compared with pre-nuclear times. Why exactly? What they mean when they refer to the atom bomb is, in fact, a social phenomenon. This is clearly discernible in the diverging behaviour of East and West Germany in this regard. Here in the GDR any thinking political human being's interest in the atom bomb does not go beyond the question of war and peace. Nobody goes to bed with the atom bomb here. Nobody goes out to buy a wardrobe and says: "Not be long before they drop the bomb I see; I'll take the cheaper one". But this behaviour is quite typical of a citizen of the Federal Republic. For the Westerner, the atom bomb is a symbol to which they can peg their social fears and uncertainties. The atom bomb is that unforeseeable cataclysm, which every member of an anarchic, crisis-stricken society sees coming at any moment. Now, finally, they have a tangible reason for this inexplicable gut feeling: a fetish. Fear crystallises around the atom bomb, the atom bomb is not the cause of this fear. The fear is much older. The fear is of great interest to art, the bomb not at all.

What was all this about the modern pace of life? Life is so mobile these days, they say. People travel with jets these days, not stagecoaches. Art needs to move with the times apparently; quicker, snappier or whatever. But such an assertion is based on sociological ideas of art, the sole function of which is to distract the science of aesthetics from the class question, and which are therefore useless. These ideas fully fail a phenomenon such as the dramatic style of Sturm und Drang.[31] The Sturm und Drang period was a

31 Sturm und Drang (Storm and Stress), literary movement of young German authors who set their subjectivity against enlightened rationalism in the 1770s.

time when the productive forces were of a truly archaic leisureliness but when the social situation was one of great tumult. Its style thus became more modern, nervous, dynamic, volatile and dialectical than that of all contemporary atom littérateurs. And jazz rhythms have really nothing to do with the rhythms of machines, their origins are entirely agrarian.

The writer who speaks about science, thus speaks about social sciences. He speaks about the social sciences of historical materialism and political economy. Perhaps, he also speaks about the social sciences of philosophy and psychology. And he should be speaking about aesthetics; because aesthetics, from Lessing to Brecht, is a German tradition, and even among German traditions, there are good ones to be found. Aesthetics improves and enriches the tools of his trade. The social sciences prepare his material such that it becomes comprehensible, manifest, feasible, in short: artistically fit for purpose. Concreteness is the child of the concept. It is seriously claimed within bourgeois circles that the world is becoming more and more complicated because science is becoming more and more complicated: the more science there is, the more complicated the world. The sciences follow the same pattern. Of course, the exact opposite is true: the more science, the more simple the world becomes; it is only complicated for common sense. [. . .]

Brecht's Aesthetics

Brecht's aesthetics is not only found in his theories or only in his plays. It resides in both and between both. The path of scientific knowledge and that of practical knowledge are two different paths; they lead to different ends, even if it's the same man who walks them. A writer who theorises usually theorises not about his art but against his art; otherwise, he could just as well leave it alone. His theory and his practice are in conflict, a conflict that stimulates him. His theories will never fully apply to his poetic work. The author always knows more than he can do, and he can always do more than he knows.

Brecht's aesthetics is a system of methods that are suitable for artistically grasping reality in its total dialectic. Any method that does this is orthodox Brechtian, even if Brecht never used it. Brecht's reality was that of the first half of the twentieth century. Our reality is already different; our methods must look different from Brecht's if they are to be Brechtian methods. Like every achievement of the human spirit, Brecht's achievement remains historical. It is impermanent and eternal. Taking it forward can only succeed through negation, not through prolongation.

Brecht's aesthetics, understood in this way, is anything but the subjective mode of practice of an eccentric genius. It applies not only to Brechtian theatre. It applies to all theatre after Brecht and to all literature and all art, and it applies to all practical human activity. The alienating attitude, i.e. the technique of concretisation through negation, is the attitude of the autonomous consciousness. The history of organic matter has recorded three leaps from the realm of necessity to the realm of freedom. The first leap is from the inanimate to the living. The second is from animal to human. The third (which we are in the process of making) is from ideologue to Marxist. Brecht's aesthetics is simply the expression of this third leap in the field of art.

Answers to 4 questions

1. Should theatre represent the contemporary world?

If it is true that art is a form of intercourse between people, then drama does not want to convey information about the world, but information about the author's attitude towards the world.

Attitudes cannot be explained; attitudes are taken on. Writers who hope that someone is interested in the views they express labour under an embarrassing misunderstanding. Nothing is of interest other than the manner in which the author masters reality in practice. The author's practice is the representation of reality.

Thus, from the premise that the purpose of drama is not representation of the world, the conclusion follows that drama must necessarily represent the world.

The reflection seems to have returned to the point of view it wanted to abandon; in truth it has already gone ahead. For the distinction, that representation of the world is not the purpose of drama but an indispensable means, is not sophistry. It has consequences of enormous practical importance.

Namely, just as surely as the dramatist is obliged to represent the world, it is no less certain that nothing obliges him to represent the entire world. Content has significance to the degree that it enables significant attitudes. Its selection is based on artistic considerations, not any other.

What is of essential concern to life may not be of concern to art at all. What object could be more worth understanding for the last seventy years than the structure of a capitalist crisis?

And yet it is futile and unproductive for art, and I wish Brecht had dealt with a less tedious subject in "Saint Joan of the Stockyards", the play in which he brings together the most brilliant of his artistic devices.

(I grumble about Brecht because the errors of the great are more productive than the errors of the minor. I could say the same about my play "Sorgen und die Macht" (Worries and the State).)

2. Can the contemporary world be represented in theatre at all?

The world of today is of course particularly resistant to attempts at depiction, but there have always been situations in reality that eluded artistic reproduction. There have also always been artists who, for non-artistic reasons, set their sights on these situations, for example all the writers of didactic poems since Hesiod. I believe a genre has its own nose. One should follow it and not try to poke it by force into anything. If one accepts that art, unlike science, has the right not to deal with all subjects, the lament about the anti-dramatic nature of modern society becomes less heartbreaking.

This is not to defend the boulevard playwrights of the West and the East, who crawl into the narrow nooks and crannies of everyday life. Drama is one of the great arts, those of which totality is demanded. The playwright is questioned about his position on the fundamental contradictions, not on the wrinkles of the surface. It remains the task of the dramatist to choose a subject matter that is productive, significant and endowed with artistic potential.

Productive subjects are always those of politically important people, since they often deal with important things and because their individual actions get magnified by the mechanisms of social amplification. Also productive as subjects are cerebral persons whose passions are novel and significant, people with philosophical feelings. Hence, what I have to offer are dramas about kings and dramas about exemplary characters.

Subjects can be found. Nonetheless, it is indeed outrageous, from the playwright's point of view, that hostile politicians are no longer related to one another, as might once have been expected of them. The three Laotian princes[32] are a notable exception.

3. What means would be suitable for this?

I think that if you have a really dramatic story, such harmless devices as, say, Shakespeare used would suffice.

4. Can it still or once again be represented by realistic means?

The question of whether the world can be represented by realistic means makes no sense at all. Means that represent the world are realistic.

One question I can understand is: should the author's attitude be reflected by realistic means? The answer, of course, depends on the attitude. Right attitudes, i.e. those that are consistent with reality, need realistic means.

Realistic art is, in plain language, an interpreted representation of reality. The difference between reality and its artistic reproduction marks the place where form comes forth, and form is the dwelling of the artist's soul. The form is the main political aspect in the work of art, i.e. what is interesting.

The artist who dares to formally master a great deal of significant reality believes that society can be humanised.

What makes the Absurdists[33] so dull is not so much the smallness of their subjects as (however closely related) the timidity of their attitudes. Sad and confused people disrupt good parties and write bad plays.

So far in this century there have been two typical directions

32 Boun Oum (1911/12–1980), Souvanna Phouma (1901–1984) and Souphanouvong (1909–1995) who represented respectively the pro-American, neutralist and communist political groups, which were involved in changing coalitions and conflicts since the Japanese occupation of Laos during the Second World War.

33 Literary current after the Second World War, which portrayed the world as lacking meaning or purpose, and thus unfathomable; represented in theatre by plays of Samuel Beckett and Eugène Ionesco.

in drama, that of Brecht and that of the Absurd. The Absurdists renounce any knowledge of the world, Brecht sacrifices everything to it. From the point of view of science, the Absurdists are wrong, and Brecht is right; from the point of view of drama they are all wrong together.

From the Foreword to the Essay "The Poetic"

Art lives from the flaws of the world. Whether it makes us laugh or cry, we laugh at or cry about things worth abolishing. Whether it depicts the world as beautiful or ugly, it demands comparison with ugly reality. The most effusive panegyric derives its zest from the fact that it implies disapproval of the inglorious. Every work of art is perfect in its own peculiar way, and perfection, as we all know, is the sister of tedium. Aesthetic perfection, however, is not tedious, it is an affront to the universe.

All art is critical, even critical art, in which the opposition in content too easily overshadows the poetic. It is precisely the most general features of artistic activity – the humanisation of the raw material, the creation of what has never existed before, the observance of self-imposed laws, coming to grips with the intractable and lending coherence to the conflicting – that bring about the interest that humanity never ceases to take in art: as in the proposal of an unalienated, productive, free life, that has been mastered and is no longer sundered by contending interests. By depicting the unsatisfactory in a satisfying way, art is itself the depiction divested of time of the relationship between problem and solution.

[. . .]

Art lives from the flaws of the world; from this it does not follow that the more flawed the world, the better art becomes. Evident distress demands a political solution, not a poetic one. Whatever is abominable needs to be eliminated, not extolled in poetry. Art, in order to be art, needs not just contradictions but a tangible unity thereof, as was the case with the Greek polis, English absolutism or – for God's sake – the German hope for a bourgeois-feudal class compromise. Such unity lifts art above the poverty of naïve partisanship and enables it to embrace the idea of totality.

Most of the works in this volume came into being after 1961, in other words, at a time when socialism was proving its ability to work well as a modern industrial society. It had begun to prove, by way of visible examples, that it was no longer merely the negation of the abominations of capitalism, but rather the sublation of its advantages: it became for the first time in practice what it had always been in theory: a system of measures for freeing the productive forces from the constrictions of private property.* The success of the GDR, reaching well beyond the century, in conjunction with its very lively contradictions, facilitated the rediscovery of art and the renewed examination of the major aesthetic questions.

Nothing in history is the same: whatever is similar, is different. The principal difference between the present time and other art-friendly periods is in regard to the fruitful contradictions between sense and nonsense; in all previous social conditions, nonsense was primary whereas today it is sense. For a long time, this good fortune caused us quite some trouble; it became our new question. How does art deal with the impeccable?

The author maintains that even the best of all actual worlds has to contain a fault: namely that it is worse than the best of all possible worlds. The object of the most recent art is, in his opinion, the relationship of utopia to reality. Utopia can exist by no other means than within a reality that is developing toward it: in so far as this is its existence, it no longer exists as such. The only achievable state of perfection of reality is the process of becoming perfect, in other words, an imperfect state.

This friendly enmity of the conceivable to the achievable gives rise to an endless number of riddles, some cheerful, some sad, mostly cheerful in fact. We can afford to be insatiable because we are no longer hungry. High performance is alienated by even higher demand. The unworthy temporary solution gets better marks than the worthy solution, which claims to be the definitive solution. Sensuality (one of the most popular themes of art in the GDR) is described in its threefold form as actual happiness, disturbing the order and the anticipation of utopia. For us, the individual (the most significant socialist accomplishment) is never emancipated enough and, at the same time, never social enough.

The author is fragmentary on this point, contenting himself to indicate a direction only. He accuses the world of being, and insofar as he makes this accusation, which is in fact a compliment, he knows that art has a secure future.

* The author would like to be unambiguous on this particular question. He has never, not even during the so-called economic miracle, ever raised any greater objection against capitalism than its incapacity to produce. How else should you call it, when a society rarely utilises more than half of its steel capacity, when it encounters the possibilities of new instruments of production (such as nuclear and control technology) with helpless ineptitude, when it has to spawn war and fascism every 25 years in parallel cycles, just so as to not drown in its own ill-distributed grease? You call that production? All other evils – militarism, oppression, obligation to lie publicly – are consequences of the one fundamental evil: its backward relations of production. With Socialism it was the exact opposite, even during its period of accumulation. It is akin to the new secretary from the old joke, who, when asked by the boss during a dictation if she can write in shorthand, replies: yes, but it is a little slower, of course.

The Entrance March of Demetrius Or: Theatre as Pomp

Any material that you examine for its dramatic possibilities has some productive aspects that leap out at you, so to speak. Whether it is a memorable character, an imbroglio that immediately reveals the rich yield that its dramaturgical treatment could bring out, a constellation that has the elements to educe a total idea of the world, or simply a compelling scene: it is these aspects that move the author to decide in favour of the material and begin the laborious handiwork of dissecting, sifting and assembling. One such aspect plays a decisive role in Schiller's reflections on "Demetrius": the entrance march of the false tsar in Moscow. Schiller notes right at the start:

> Onlookers on the roofs and gates as the false Demetrius enters. – The pontoon bridge to Moscow, over this a triumphal arch. Down a long street can be seen painted spectators standing shoulder to shoulder, on windows and roofs too. – This opulent sight of the jostling crowds of people must at once strike the eye when the curtain goes up.

Under the heading "Pro", the poet collects the arguments in support of the Demetrius material. He writes:

> The material is promising because of its many sensual and sometimes magnificent portrayals. Among them stand out: the entrance into Moscow and the Tsar's wedding, but especially the passage from a joyous celebration to a murderous one. In addition to these, there are also aspects of brutal tsarist violence, murderous deeds, battles, victories, ceremonies, and so on.

One must know that the late Schiller cannot be fully appreciated but as a forerunner of nineteenth-century drama. His dramaturgy of intrigue introduces the line of Scribe – Birch-Pfeiffer. With the "Bride of Messina", but first and foremost "The Children of the House", he invents the restoration drama of fate before Müllner and before Houwald. The "Maid of Orleans" in turn initiates the romantic pageant of Auffenberg or Holbein.

The coronation procession in the "Maid" was appreciated as the most splendid and imitated countless times. The report on a successful performance of the "Maid" in Breslau (in Winkler's Repertoire) boils down to the following single sentence: "Never before did the coronation procession of about three hundred people appear here with such resplendence". This throws light on why Schiller repeatedly mentions the procession of Demetrius among the standing scenes, and also why all the thinking that he still has to do on the scene is centred on how to distinguish this procession from the one in the "Maid". He writes:

> Entrance into Moscow
>
> The main scene of the play in light of what is of interest as material.
>
> Backdrop of the city of Moscow; even as one looks, it is transformed into an immense throng of houses and towers in the distance; half the front curtain is similarly decorated, here and there the glimmer of a few gold-plated cupolas. Closer up and in the stage settings, one espies spectators gazing from windows and roofs and scaffoldings. A pontoon bridge over the Moskva may appear, thereby duplicating the procession . . .
>
> In order that this scene does not converge with the coronation procession in the "Maid of Orleans", it must be directed and arranged in a wholly different way . . .
>
> It can be arranged differently by adding a bridge or a triumphal arch, by the more numerous presence of spectators and the populace on the roofs and towers, by the procession itself, with richly decorated horses and the Tsar too on horseback.

You have to laugh. The example is banal. In order to show that this, like all other banal examples, demonstrates the general laws of art, albeit in a naive, crude, and predictable way, let me remind you of a different kind of parade: the parades of metaphors in the great Shakespearean monologues.

> Now is the winter of our discontent
> Made glorious summer by this sun of York;
> And all the clouds that lour'd upon our house
> In the deep bosom of the ocean buried.

Here, as in a romantic pageant, the dressed-up extras and the dressed-up thoughts march in long, close succession, and it would be idle to claim that this linguistic splendour is merely a means to a more exalted undertaking and not an end in itself. By the way, let me say in passing, a metaphor is an inherently poetic thing. Unlike the allegory and the parable, which allude to a specific single event, a metaphor denotes an indefinite multitude of instances of a similar kind. It declares the analogy it makes to be applicable in multiple ways. This means, however, that it scours the world in quest of enduring, constant and repetitive phenomena.

We have come from the digressive to the synoptic and then, maybe, back to the topic. The suspicion arises, of course, that the poetic has a special proclivity for what is worthless and that its fraught relationship with the here and now makes it particularly prone to turn into kitsch. The suspicion, I believe, is deceptive. The here and now is no less distant from a large, comprehensive perspective than the there and never, and more harm is caused by the kitsch based on facts, the factual jumble and the documentary, this realism of the common man, than by poetic kitsch. False poetry can hardly be as inconsequential as false prose. Alienation presents us with a choice between dematerialising the human and dehumanising the material. We do not accept this choice, but we consider the latter failing to be the more critical, perhaps because it is the more current one. Incidentally, it is this failing that brought poetry under the aforesaid suspicion. But no category is more suspect than that of the pompous.

To define the word conceptually, pomp is the coincidence of the sensual with the ceremonial. Pomp flaunts itself or is show; pomp becomes a feast for the eyes and ears as soon as it has a festive, stately character. The pompous is not a concept superordinate to the poetic in the sense that what is poetic must be pompous, but a partial concept: what is characterised by pomp is poetic. The deployment of pomp befits the poetic and makes it vibrant. When I speak of poetry, I certainly do not speak of prayers and still less of chaste maids; I leave such delicate matters to the Sunday papers. I am concerned with saving what is worth saving and elaborating a theory of realism in which the classical finally has a place once again. The classical is poetic and the classical is marked by pomp.

Classical eras are always those of the theatre. Classical eras for the novel are non-classical eras. I delineate the pompous with reference to theatre, because in theatre it is not only possible – as in all poetic genres – but rather indispensable.

The structural laws of genres depend on the sociological structure of the audience, which they are intended to appeal to. Of all the arts, theatre is the most public and convivial; all the world knows it, but not all the world is attuned to it. Time and again, some people turn up who leave their instruments in the outhouse and their cloaks and daggers in the closet and then boast that they have improved the theatre by doing away with it. Is it so difficult to appreciate that the need to reach a good many people, who are distant both in terms of thoughts and space, requires a certain elevation of the level of performance, of gestures and hence also of the emotional and intellectual attitude?

Theatre is not a quiet business. The performance begins emphatically; not with a whimper but a bang. Shakespeare's trumpet and flag (or later, in a closed house, the lighting of the stage lamps), the opening ballad in old Spanish theatre, the three knocks of French classical theatre: all these starting signals serve to silence the audience, but also to announce that what follows will be worth the silence of so many people. Our "bang" is the ceremonial rising of the red plush curtain. There are reformers who recommend that the red curtain be eliminated or exchanged for substitute fabrications made of materials from the real world around us. They argue that this is necessary for the struggle against what is old-fashioned and for the avowal of reality. But I fear the real motive is no better than a lack of a sense of personal worth.

The king, with his purple cloak and his golden cardboard crown, still figures as a symbol of the theatre. He is as irreplaceable as the plush curtain; that is, he is irreplaceable unless one has recognised his function. The king is not just the president of old times. Unlike the president, the king belongs in the realm of poetry. He too, it is true, is a socially powerful and privileged agent of action. At the same time, however, as someone of high standing and importance on a world scale, he represents human beings in their most extreme manifestation. Whatever he may be, scoundrel, statesman, weakling, father, lover or wise man, he is so in the highest degree. He suffers and determines not only his own fate but that of his people; hence, the theatre, like the fairy tale, makes him a symbol of human grandeur. There is nothing nonhuman about him, he is rather the most human of human beings. The red carpet is rolled out in front of him, and he fully deserves it.

Pomp became an object of disparagement because it appeared as mere hollow spectacle in the reified, soulless world of the bourgeoisie. But, as far as I can see, there can be nothing against expressing great things in a grand way. Seen historically, theatre as pomp is an expression of the self-confidence of a class. Aesthetically understood, it is a celebration of human potential, an exuberant display of what has been attained and is attainable, of human pride and self-esteem.

Art and Revolution

It is common knowledge that communists differ from the swarms of pipe-dreamers in that they are able to think about what happens the day after the revolution.

It is common knowledge that communists will not content themselves with the eradication of bourgeois society: they are, in fact, concerned with the establishment of a socialist and, thereafter, a communist society.

It is common knowledge that socialist society is not inferior to bourgeois society, it is superior.

And it is not unknown that communists do not wish to cast away the treasures of goods and abilities that have been accumulated by the obsolete classes. Rather, they will appropriate them and develop them to a higher level.

The inventions of the bourgeoisie, for example: reason, individual love, spiritual freedom, wealth.

What, then, should prevent them from taking hold of art, which the bourgeoisie has abandoned, along with reason, individual love and spiritual freedom? Indeed, what should prevent them from taking hold of the wealth to which the bourgeoisie clings so dearly?

In fact, they are unoriginal enough to retain what is useful and not what is useless.

What case is there against the usefulness of art? By way of its unique capacity to subjectively process material, art proposes the humanisation of the world. This certainly renders art useless to the bourgeoisie. But why should that be the case for communists?

The human being, as an individual, is presented with the possibility of emancipation. The workers, as a class, are presented with the possibility of emancipation. Humankind in history is presented with the possibility of emancipation. You can see this unless, of course, you see the world the way imperialism would have you believe it to be.

The content of art is, perhaps, the present that is sick with imperialism. We, at once, are the form.

The revolution commits its fatal flaw when it understands itself purely in terms of its relationship to imperialism, and thus sticks to it as its inverse, its mirror image and its hypnotised negation.

The father of this bourgeois counter-culture was Leo Tolstoy. One fine, senile day he suddenly had his fill of decadence and became instead anti-decadent. He tumbled out of all the nonsense he had defended until then, only to tumble into the opposite nonsense.

Because art was once beautiful and useless, it ought now to be useful and ugly. Because one once had form without content, there ought now to be content without form. Because those who appreciated art were idlers, art ought now to be guided by those who do not actually appreciate it.

But the rear end of decadence is no less decadent than its nose.

Tolstoy's son was called Zhdanov, his grandson Mao.

Admittedly, art is a weapon. Admittedly, a mallet is a weapon. According to Aristotle, it does not follow, that art must be a mallet.

Rather, it follows that art is all the better a weapon, the more artistic it is.

Everything else is not revolutionary theory, but the theory of despondency about the revolution.

Whoever talks about *crisis*, talks about their own crisis. Communists have concerns and are not in crisis, nor will they heed the advice of those who recommend they write poor verse.

Butzbach Author Survey

Dear Mr. Müller (and dear students), all your questions can be answered in one sentence, which I have unfortunately already said somewhere: I am in favour of literature that isn't politically committed by authors who are politically committed.

By that, I mean three things.

First, that art is not very well suited to exercise direct political influence. There are circumstances where it must try but what comes out is usually bad art.

Second, that a writer, like every human being, is incomplete and stunted if he neglects to behave politically. Put simply, I believe a responsible citizen of the 20th century should be a communist and act as such.

And thirdly, that an artist inevitably expresses his being in his art and consequently a communist artist, whatever he may talk about, cannot at all do otherwise than make communist art.

So much for that. You are right, an artist tends to come into conflict with society. This has been intrinsic to the profession ever since there has been art. Not only does he come into conflict with opposing classes; he just as necessarily comes into conflict with the class to which he feels affiliated. I repeat: it was never different; it is inherent to the profession. The solution is theoretically very simple: under no circumstances must he betray art, and under no circumstances must he betray progress. How does he do this practically? As well he can.

Sincerely yours, Peter Hacks

Saving Christianity from the Christians (Excerpt from "On 'Adam and Eve'"[34])

[. . .] The God of religion may well be paler than the mythical tribal king. But, in the sheer scope of his conception, he is worth far more than the king who was really just a God of development. His internal contradictions are immeasurably more interesting than the king's holy caprices. It would be petty to deny his existence, especially now that the Christians are so set on it.

In general, one of the tasks of Marxist art is to save Christianity from the Christians.

One has to admit that Christianity tends toward bashfulness, more so than other religions. It is wary of the judgement of reason as a prude is wary of common gossip. And it grows all the more prudish as it grows older, making the most unbelievable sacrifices for the sake of its reputation.

At first, Christians were embarrassed about their mythological and polytheistic origins. Anybody travelling over land at that time could chance across the Madonnas flung by Christians out of the churches and onto the dung heaps. This could still suit artists well enough. They gathered up the old mother goddesses and exhibited them in their cabinets of curiosities.

Of late, however, artists even stumble across the Holy Spirit, the Son and not infrequently the Father himself when wandering over dung heaps. The Christians themselves had cast them out. They have reduced Christianity to a couple of sentences about justice, virtue and the creation of a dignified world. All of which, may God be the author's witness, Marxists understand better.

Of course, Christians are burdened with the difficulty of believing in something that is not actually true. Alas, that is the precondition of their ferment and if they wish to carry on, they have

34 Essay by Hacks about his play 'Adam und Eva'.

to make their peace with it. The other road is a dead-end. They do their best to root what is untrue out of their teachings. And as a consequence, they are in the process of rooting the Christianity out of Christianity. [. . .]

Christianity is not true in the sense that its teachings are based on actual events or that its beliefs are actually reasonable. The truth of it is only accessible to those who do not believe it to be true. Whoever is not obliged to believe it can make some use of it. This is why the artists, having found God in distress after being cast out from the house of God, were quite willing, albeit after some initial embarrassment, to take the fine and diaphanous old man under their wing.

Even in this, Goethe was ahead of them; the value and exemplary character of the "Faust II" finale[35] cannot be praised highly enough. Thanks to Goethe, humanity knows – yesterday's religion is today's art.

The business is, as the saying goes, mutually beneficial. There remains a posthumous abode for religion thanks to aesthetic consciousness. It is to aesthetic consciousness that it owes its immortality. Art, in turn, was bequeathed a substantial heritage of poetically formulated reality by religion, which, in its lifetime, saw itself as an explanation of the world. By no means, then, does the author have in mind only those beauteous facets of Christianity that should be retained. What he expressly intends to talk about is what could be retained of its insights.

The insights of a mythical or mythically influenced dialectic are, of course, pre-scientific in nature; this does not mean they are redundant. Science does not know everything. And what it does know is nowhere near being useful to art. As far as practical judgement goes, the sensual means of comprehending, which changes not only the head but the stance of he who comprehends, frequently obtains richer and more accurate results. [. . .]

35 'Faust': play by Goethe in two parts.

Note on Young Writers in the GDR

These people have not lived under capitalism. The individual, the writer in particular, has only what he has experienced or acquired through his own efforts. Study cannot replace this. [They are all against capitalism, honestly, and their elders cannot understand why they do not act accordingly.] The former have lived under socialism and, quite naturally, they write only about this; critically. It would be quite normal if socialism's contradictions were the principal contradiction. But the principle contradiction is that between socialism and capitalism. For those who know capitalism, this is quite clearly and naturally not just a matter of knowledge. But whoever only knows of it through books does not have the requisite total disgust, the disgust that has passed into attitudes and stabilised in them, which is necessary to emotionally subordinate the displeasure at deficiencies here to this disgust. So they engage in opposition. They have a lot of advantages over their elders; nice, funny and unsentimental young people. Disadvantage: frighteningly clueless on questions of Marxism.

Information for America (Excerpt)

1. What is the function of literature in socialism?

The function of art is the same at all times and in all places. Using aesthetic means and for aesthetic purposes, it examines contemporary reality for the possibilities it offers the human species in its process of self-creation. From its special position in society, it puts forward the perfect human being. It does this by discarding whatever is inhibitive and envisioning what is worth striving for. In the mixing of these two processes, the accent in the GDR is on envisioning, not discarding. As such, our literature has less in common with the literature of Webster, Swift or Bierce; it is rather faced with challenges similar to those of Sophocles, Shakespeare or Goethe.

2. What contemporary social problems am I particularly concerned with?

What socialism has to achieve is emancipation: currently, that of women and that of the gifted individual. This is what my state is concerned with, and this is what my writing is concerned with.

3. Does my work take into account the topic of "women in society"?

The woman is a type of person that also concerns me in a non-aesthetic context. In terms of the subject matter of my dramas, perhaps that is my main subject. Socialism, which is the first modern society to have achieved full legal emancipation for women, is a vast experiment in the future disposition of women. Like all experiments mankind undertakes on itself, this experiment too demands appalling costs. I'm not referring to financial losses but to the agony and turmoil of souls. In order to reduce these costs, it is most necessary to accompany the practical experiment with knowledge, both scientific and artistic. So far, one thing is certain: for the sexes to have identical dispositions is neither achievable nor desirable. What is required is to develop male and female – of course not rigid – role behaviour. But what the right role for women (and men) might look like, and how to solve the problem of difference without superiority and inferiority, no one knows to this day, and I devote a large part of my efforts in helping to figure it out.

4. What influence would my youthful experiences have had on my work?

I came into being in very favourable times and under very favourable circumstances. As a child growing up in an anti-fascist family, I got to know imperialism in its most explicit form, as Nazism. As an adolescent, that is, at the age when one thinks most, I experienced liberation in West Germany as a happily undefined offer of all kinds of suggestions and hopes; and in the years, in which one may begin to call oneself a man, I found enough reasons to decide in favour of Communism. I believe the age groups before and after me had less leeway to learn about human prospects and less grounds to believe in any prospects for human beings at all.

5. How did I gain experience with workers and what relationship do I have with them today?

Of course, for professional reasons, I made efforts to get to know the working class, like all other classes. I think I know it, though I don't live with it.

6. What are the special features of GDR literature within the German-speaking area?

GDR literature, well, it's better. It's not that our writers were born with abler minds than their peers across the border. Nor is it mainly due to the fact that the great representatives of German literature were in the GDR and exerted their influence here as teachers and examples. The reason, I think, is that the difficulties created by capitalism for making art do not arise in the GDR. One such difficulty, for example, is the difficulty of saying anything new in the bourgeois world. There is nothing new to be said about imperialism; it is aesthetically finished; what can be said about it, has already been said.

[Ideal and Utopia]

In principle, I prefer the notion of the ideal to utopia: partly because we possess it individually, partly because of the misuse made of the word utopia by all those who are born to be wrong. The ideal is a desirable thing that doesn't exist and which, it is readily admitted, will not exist in any place or time; it is, therefore, a scientific and materialist concept. The wrong ways of dealing with the concept of utopia can hardly be fully enumerated. It is often taken for something ostensibly implementable, as in *Freedom Now* or *Communism here*; such nonsense, even if it behaves like a terrorist, is a utopia born of weakness and nothing better than the red degeneration of the blue flower. There is also utopia out of malice, namely when an undesirable thing that exists (such as the state of affairs in the USA) is declared a utopia by people like Orwell or Huxley, simply by prolonging it into the future. Common among socialists is utopia in a trivial sense, i.e. the use of the name for desired successes such as world peace. But world peace is not a utopia. It is a goal, and goals carry less weight in art than hopes. Real ideals are the all-round educated human being or *To each according to his needs*[36] or the equality of the sexes; they lie in the future and at the same time nowhere; we know we will never get there, and yet we always have to want to get there.

36 From each according to his ability, to each according to his needs! – slogan representing for Marx the higher phase of communist society after the phase of socialism.

Foreword to the Essay "Determinations"

Art approaches the world, the work of art makes a statement, but a statement about what? Not about the world, but about the artist's approach to the world. By the world we understand with good reason nothing else and nothing stranger than humankind; thus, art simultaneously brings news about humanity and the human being. Again, for any news, there have to be two sides: the one who brings it and the one who receives it, or the artist and the audience. From this it finally follows: by means of the artistic knowledge embodied in the work of art, humanity comes to an understanding, mediated via the artist, with humanity, mediated via the audience, about how best to approach humanity, mediated via the object, and come to terms with itself. The study of humanity is humanity. Art is the trinity of the world spirit. Art poses a higher question than science; because it asks about the whole, which alone is true. Both the world and with it, the most masterly manner of approaching this world change or even advance. But approaches are more likely to change than advance; in mundane reality a technique is lost as soon as we make use of the next; only in the high realm of art do we have all the conceptions of the mind next to each other. From the chances afforded by many eras, art puts together a repertoire of diverse and yet enduring proposals relevant for the free, mature human being who has learned to master his fate. Art is inalienable and unsurpassable because it always deals with the same content. The content of all art is the perfect human being, an ideal.

The tools of art are the genres. They are tried and tested and, like the object for which they are intended, they are inalienable and unsurpassable. The world can be grasped in its essence, not in its completeness; the genre chooses apposite segments from things and settings. The work of art and the animal take possession of the material of the world, and both do this by virtue of the separation into species: the kind of material that it devours is figured and by then prefigured in its structural design and the shape of its teeth. The question of genres coincides with the question of realism. The audience, if it is to be set in motion, must be touched at all the vital points of the nerves and muscles that induce human beings to turn to the world; these are the senses, brain, heart, instincts, stimuli; and this has to happen in the groups to which the audience flocks in consideration of the particular terrain. The audience approves by going along. The logic of taste judges in the form of enjoyment. As soon as the artist seizes the world by means of the genres, he already has it as a part that represents the whole, and he has already prepared it for an audience that, though distinct in class and education, stands for history that has to come to reason. There is a suitable tool for every subdomain. There are the major genres: the arts, and there are their varieties and sub-varieties. The genres act as a guarantor for the suitability of the approach; indeed, that is what matters; the making is, in fact, the thing. Whoever wants the work must want the tools. Whoever doesn't want the work, the author of this book doesn't want anything from them. Art without genres is also a way of approaching the world, namely the wrong way. Its content is the unhappy human being, who more often than not is simply the real and clumsy human being.

Whoever paints a turnip, paints, whether intentionally or not, the ideal. Art has form; form is the distribution of weights, hence form of something; it requires a content, which is then what it means. The form of the work of art is, on the one hand, the form of the world; it is, on the other hand, the form of the approach, or (as the scholars would say) the kinetic habitus, the gait. This only succeeds if it is in the form of a genre; but succeeding, that is luck. The genre form becomes a beautiful form, a form as such, it appears as an ideal form and ultimately as the form of the ideal. The concept of art is so rich, the entirety of the mediations, reactions and interactions contained in it so entangled, that there is not a sentence about art that is not true. All sentences are correct and all are too little. Therefore, it is not too difficult to say what art is, but too easy. All definitions of the aesthetic are only in order to amuse oneself. Thinking about art works best as an attempt at a morphology of the arts: as thinking about genres; if you understand the tool, you pretty much understand the product. Art, the author thinks, is the imitation by means befitting the genre of an object suited to the genre. The author concedes, however, that the best definition demands some goodwill. The human being, for instance, is much less composed than art and much easier to define. The school of Plato very aptly defined him as a two-legged animal without feathers, as an animal that is, and as one that distinguishes itself by the upright walk and by nakedness, i.e. need for clothing, housing, heating, in short, civilisation. For them, the barrel thinker Diogenes brought a plucked rooster into the lecture hall that also wanted to be a human being. The most tiresome joke is found among logicians. You may be as specific as you want, there's always someone who'll come with plucked roosters.

The author has thought about a few of the more modest genres: poetry, opera, fairy tales for children, ballads, pornography. He hasn't thought about the genre of drama; this is too difficult for him; because he knows it much too well.

From the Essay "Poetic Commerce"

ANCIENT TRADE

The Out-of-Timeness of Art Production

How much does art cost, and why does it cost what it costs?

The question is not easy and can be considered unresolved. It is perhaps advisable to confront it with naiveté and as it appears; the author takes a look at artists as they wade through life and trade their wares. The works of art themselves are expensive, hardly anyone can afford one. On the other hand, the effort that the artists put into creating them seems not very impressive. One encounters the most humble conditions there.

A poet has a room with a desk and dictionaries. A composer has a room with a desk and a piano. A painter has a large room with a large north-facing window. A sculptor's equipment is handsome in comparison. He lives in a kind of barn with a tool shelf and a couple of sack barrows and pulleys; things are almost as grand as at a blacksmith's place.

Production does not increase by enlarging the workshop. Two writers working together would have two rooms, two desks and two copies of the Dornseiff lexicon[37]; nothing would be gained. Downsizing would be more feasible. One can save on the room and the paraphernalia if it comes down to that. Some are known to have written poems on the margins of newspapers. Nor does production increase through the introduction of new implements; the growth of the productive forces has bypassed the production of art without touching it. The development from the pen to the computer has not accelerated the writing of poetry. Poetry has not changed as a result, it is no more beautiful and, astonishingly enough, no less beautiful.

37 Reference work of German vocabulary sorted by subject groups.

A gem is still cut with the same tools that Pyrgoteles used for cutting. A bronze is cast using exactly the same techniques that Myron used for casting.

Even the theatre, which requires levers, boards and lamps, and several artists who have to be exhorted to tolerate each other, has not suffered any changes since its origins. It is well known that theatre was at times more expensive than at other times. But if theatre means that a real play is staged properly by the right number of actors for an audience, then nothing has changed in the efforts expended on a performance since Sophocles except the amount of money thrown away each time.

Making music, that is: someone brings a device and makes the air vibrate with it. This is how it is today, and it was no different in the days when Jubal performed at Jabal's wedding.

THE MULE

Preliminary Definition of the Economic Genre

When artists are finished with their work of art, they go and sell it to their buyers, to those who enjoy art. A buyer can also be a reprographic company, to which the artist acts as the supplier. In both cases we are dealing with the micro-production of goods.

In both cases, the situation is such that the artist, as his own employer, engages himself as his own wage labourer; he fulfills the criteria of a working entrepreneur. He, too, creates surplus value by working and likes doing so all the more since he is the one who takes it away from himself. Marx does not promise a long life to such androgynous producers. Economic development, he says in "Theories of Surplus Value" (Appendix f), is averse to their puzzling activities and makes sure that this group of exploiters of their own power is split into a few proper exploiters and many who are properly exploited. As far as art is concerned, there is no indication that development has succeeded in doing this. But it is easy to see that very few goods have been produced in a comparable way since the invention of industry.

For this reason, the founders of classical political economy approach art without much enthusiasm. When they do, it is never without irritation. We value Marx not least for his ability to express ire. Where he deals with artists, we can count on him. "These fellows. . ." it goes, "these lackeys. . ." ("Theories" IV). "Now the shit at last gets soulful". Marx, in fact, loved the arts, but he did not love them in his capacity as an economist.

It is a constant observation that all sciences regard with distaste those parts of the world that are guilty of functioning in accordance with a logic other than that envisaged for them. It is true that science cannot decapitate recalcitrant facts as a real lawmaker could and would. But it can nonetheless ban them as inferior realities, as *undesirable facts*, from the realm of what is worthy of knowledge.

The author will try at least to explain such violations of the law with the law. The main forms of travel today are surely highways, which are used by automobiles. But if one has business on top of a high and not too frequented mountain, one may prefer to use a mule, just as one would have six thousand years ago. The same applies to the forms of passage in the scientifically figurative sense. They may dominate as much as they want. But wherever there's still a bridle path, there's still a mule.

In the few places where art appears in the works of classical political economy, it appears out of place in time and as an exception. For humanity, unlike the economy, art is not an exception. It is a good that has been produced since our race existed; always in the same and, therefore, probably the right way.

If at all we wish to talk about this economic exception, then it must be possible to set the exception as the rule and thus to grasp the production of art not simply as a break in time, but as a separate set of economic rules. Be it antiquated when measured against the more flexible modes of production, be it insignificant when compared to the large-scale forms of manufacture: it is what it is and worth discussing for what it is. A mule is not fully described by stating that it is not a motor vehicle.

A form of production, which is determined by the product – this is what the author calls, an economic genre.

A genre is something difficult to change. It is a way of handling any object so that what is impelled by the object is primary and what is impelled by society secondary. A genre stays the same or similar throughout history.

An economic genre (or for those who sense a slight exaggeration of the claim in scholarly terms: an appropriate form of any enterprise) aims at a specific use value. This is the optimal way to obtain it. In an economy based on commodity production, progress is just another word for cost reduction; the lower the value, the more advanced the commodity. But there are two ways in which we can talk about the production of goods: we can determine whether the method of production is advanced or whether it is suitable. With certain goods it is not pointless to enquire about their usability. Art, for example, is better viewed from the standpoint of use value.

Works of art are made by individuals who may call in a few assistants – typists or paint makers – though they could just as well dispense with them. Their methods of production, though immensely sophisticated, require harmless tools, far more harmless than those of most other artisans. Since the artist cannot eat the works of art, it stands to reason that he intends to offer them for exchange. So there's a lot to be said for the assumption that the creation of art simply belongs to the category of oddballs. The author will follow this assumption and see where he lands. For the time being, he defines the economic genre of art production as a case of small commodity production. The author doubts whether he will be able to maintain this definition in the long term. But at any rate, it's a definition; as long as it applies, it applies.

[. . .]

ON CERTAIN ERRORS IN MARX AND ENGELS

The Uniqueness of the Work of Art, Disputation

[. . .]

It was not just Marx and Engels who went to the Hegel school. Plenty of other youngsters carved their names on the school desks next to theirs and every one of them, in his own particular way, had misunderstood the teacher. "The German Ideology", apart from being a revolutionary work of genius, is also a sort of schoolboys' brawl. Max Stirner took the biggest walloping. He was the benchmate, who, as far as free listening goes, had made the most exceptional accomplishments.

Hegel taught that history is in constant movement and that it will eventually culminate in reason. History is, according to Hegel, a broadly assembled and indeed rather clumsy body that demands a significant period of time in order to fully fulfill itself, heaving from one side to another as it does so. There is no more realistic a philosophy than this. It deals with the conditions of freedom. Of all this, however, freedom was the only word to have penetrated Stirner's own egocentric ear, and he became an abolisher of states, an enemy of the law; an anarchist.

In the meantime, Marx and Engels revealed why history is constantly in movement. They related every phenomenon on earth to the growth of the forces of production and their inclinations and aversions regarding the relations of production. It is fair to say that, in their passion for discovery, they overstepped the line now and again. Indeed, in battle, even the truth is bellicose and excessive. The clearest and most profound intellectual source can tear asunder the banks of many a serene shore, which one would have done better to leave well alone.

So, along with a number of well-deserved slaps, Stirner also gets quite a few for claiming that artistic work is "unique labour" and for his "haggling for an additional wage" for this "unique labour", as well as for claiming that "If you are in a position to afford joy to thousands of people, then thousands will remunerate you for it; for it is in your power not to do it". Marx and Engels did not suffer from Stirner's inferiority complex. Indeed, his perennial upper-case "I" or "Ego" must have seriously gotten on their nerves. No doubt they also fought over their classmate's failure to appreciate the paramount importance of simple labour in creating value. Today's playwright, on the other hand, who earns exactly ten times as much from a hundred thousand readers as from ten thousand and exactly ten times as much from a hundred thousand theatre-goers as from ten thousand, cannot quite understand why they should speak with such contempt on the matter.

For Stirner, the work of art is entirely unique and this, he says, is why it is so expensive. Raphael and Mozart are his examples. Marx and Engels grumble curtly that the elevated price had already been explained by Adam Smith. The author can only regret that they did not indicate where.

Do they really mean to boil the price of a Raphael down to the value of skilled labour? Would they then be willing to recognise as a surcharge the value added for his having been sold valuable knowledge of the vanishing point by Pietro Perugino? Or are they alluding to the following section in Smith: "Such enhancements of the market price are evidently the effect of natural causes, which may hinder the effectual demand from ever being fully supplied" ("Wealth of Nations" 1–7)? There is a very real danger they have the former, and not this Smith in mind.

Now caught up in the fray, Raphael bears the brunt of so many angry slaps aimed at Stirner, and is dispatched with Stirner. Even Raphael's art is socially determined, they state. Nobody is denying that, it just does not change anything. The renaissance was to no avail, the value of the renaissance is not absorbed by renaissance art. The reason we pay such a high price for renaissance art is solely its ideas. As Alexandre Dumas so graciously says about the renaissance, "Men were giants in those times" ("Twenty Years After"). The Renaissance made painters of some Italians and of most Italian painters good painters. But even the Renaissance only made of Raphael a Raphael.

But it all boils down to one thing; "Sancho" Stirner must be wrong. "As always", claim our bickering school chums, "Sancho is again unlucky with his practical examples. He thinks that 'no one can compose your music for you, complete the sketches for your paintings. No one can do Raphael's works for him'. Sancho could surely have known, however, that it was not Mozart himself, but someone else who composed the greater part of Mozart's Requiem and finished it, and that Raphael himself 'completed' only an insignificant part of his own frescoes". As was later only rarely the case, Marx and Engels were unlucky with their practical examples here. Dealing with Stirner makes them quite sloppy.

By coincidence, both Mozart and Raphael died at a rather young age and we could have got over their untimely demise all the easier had those assistants who had allegedly slaved at their work until then only come out of hiding and continued to work as their successors. So why did Raphael's assistants serve Raphael as assistants and not the other way around? Why was their artistry extinguished on the day of his death? (The author's endeavour here is to make himself understood by those who would not lose much sleep over the loss of one particular artist. If he cannot do it, their logic goes, somebody else will. But this hope can be legitimately declared debunked. Somebody else cannot do it).

You have to be really academically uninformed about any type of creative activity to not know the difference between a genius and his sidekick. Still under thirty in 1845, Marx and Engels were in full possession of their faculties, though not yet in full possession of scientific socialism. On top of that, Marx could write poetry and Engels could draw. They did not rule out the possibility that their work might well replace that of others. Whatever reasons they saw for division of labour, they did not see in themselves. Exhilarated by their youthful all-round talents, they felt all work could be replaced. It speaks for the hearts of our young Marxists that they presumed every member of their race, onetime apprentices included, to be no less capable than themselves. But it does not speak for their knowledge of the world.

[...]

THE ARTWORKS OF THE PORTER

Creative Work

The author cannot fail to criticise the fact that Marx and Engels ascribed, on the one hand, an excessively constrained mode of producing art to the past, present and near future and predicted, on the other hand, an excessively unrestrained one for the distant future. Their deadline was the beginning of communism. Until that certain day, they tell us, nothing can work for the individual, from then on everything will. As for the outlook for art, there is a difference of opinion between Eugen Dühring and Friedrich Engels here. It can be found in "Anti-Dühring", (II-6).

Dühring, incapable of differentiation we recall, reproaches Marx for his educated arrogance and his inability to relinquish "the spectre of skilled labour time". Dühring himself claims to be unbiased enough to "recognise the labour-time of a porter and that of an architect as of absolutely equal value from the standpoint of economics".

Is that so hard to contest? It would seem so. Engels avoids getting into the question of the "economic worth" of skilled labour. He dodges. Skilled labour, he counters, is the spawn of capitalism. Skilled labour, and the division of labour along with it, will be entirely redundant under communism. This must (and does) mean that under communism every worker can do every job.

Engels furiously defends Marx against the accusation of erudition. Posing as a far better friend of ordinary people, he throws back at Dühring the charge of educated arrogance.

For Herr Dühring, he declares scornfully, it would be "monstrous" at best, "that in times to come there will no longer be any professional porters or architects, and that the man who for half an hour gives instructions as an architect will also act as a porter for a period, until his activity as an architect is once again required".

Honestly, two men of the people. You can just see the slouch hats and red sashes. Like something from the Hambach festival. And yet, none of the three of them, neither Marx and Engels nor Dühring, could be suspected of having ever pushed a porter's cart. But there is no doubt about it, Engels' argumentation is clouded by memories of youthful exuberance spent with Marx. "The German Ideology" ("Saint Max") had actually claimed that in those more wondrous times to come "the subordination of the individual to some definite art" – i.e. being an artist by profession – will disappear. "In a communist society there are no painters but only people who engage in painting among other activities."

The present author, who himself has neither time nor inclination to push carts, cannot help but wonder how it is to be an architect for half an hour. Engels' principle error lies in his far too casual conclusion that a specialised skill is by its very nature a form of domination and thus never conditioned by individual inclinations or professional requirements; in fact, it's simply the result of capitalist class divisions. Hence his particular enthusiasm for the disposable.

Disposable means being available. How on earth could anybody be enthusiastic about availability? Is not the de-skilling of labour a strategy of the most highly developed capitalism to threaten the cheapest of labour with still cheaper labour and deploy the reserve army at any time and in any place of exploitation it wishes?

Marx characterises (in Capital III, II-10) the power of factories to turn goldsmiths into mere gold-beaters (and architects into house-beaters. . .) as follows.

"Indifference of the labourer to the nature of his labour. The greatest possible reduction of labour in all spheres of production to simple labour. The elimination of all vocational prejudices among labourers." This is quite a dreadful process. All the more dreadful when it is praised as "self-realisation".

Marxism really should find some way of getting its youthful followers off its back. – The Marxian blueprint of abolishing the division of labour right up to abolishing specialist talents and specialist knowledge was perused by John Dewey, USA, and exported back to Europe. The only products that the Americans are still lucky enough to export are those of evil spirits. The broad appeal that, of all things, this isolated part of Marxism has found, suggests that Marxism stands on shaky ground here. It is so curiously compatible with the position taken by industry. Engels tells Dühring what the culture pages in newspapers tell us today. Let us stick with art.

Industry does not employ artists, so it acts and works against their profession. Industry has the minister in hand, who has fashion in hand. Via fashion it has created a mood wherein artistic work is thought of as defamatory. But if you want to annihilate the artist, you have to annihilate art. The aesthetics of fashion teaches us that any human activity is, as such, artistic and anything produced by such activity, an artwork: you need only decide to name it as such. To bolster such an assertion, activity was baptised creativity and the works were baptised objects (The annihilated enjoyment of art, incidentally, was baptised communication).

Among those working in fashion we find professional artists whose ambition consists in concealing their skill and being able to pass themselves off as cart pushers. They are only considered to have achieved something when they find new ways of meeting the difficulties in art with ineptitude. They are then paid quite fabulous sums, not in their capacity as artists but in their capacity as slayers of art, with unsightly money, if you will.

The whole Marxian ideal of the all-rounder human being, one must fear, is the left-romantic, the anarcho-democratic idealisation of what is industrially hammered and stamped into shape. The only person fit to do everything is he who is not fit to do anything. Since we are familiar with monopolistic logic and have seen the artistic consequences of all this creativity nonsense, we are somewhat sensitive when it comes to this dream of Marx and Engels and the faulty reasoning in their whimsical utopia.

"Human", the author repeats Marx and himself, means "the labour power which, on an average, apart from any special development, exists in the organism of every ordinary individual". Marx and Engels, when they spoke seriously, used the term "human labour" as meaning "machine labour": as the term for work wherein the machine is skilled and the person manning it is unskilled and its servant. In classical political economy, a human worker is an unskilled worker.

All of a sudden "human" is translated as "creative". The word has a second meaning. An unskilled worker is now also referred to as a creative worker.

Nothing will come of this either now or hereafter, regardless of how many aeons into the future one thinks. Communism can make common property of all commodities, but not of unique works. To deny that art is unique is to deny art. Art makes neither a good hobby-horse nor a good side job, nor is it meant for the DIY movement. Incidentally, the idea of a hobby economics does not inspire any trust. Even the most childish and superfluous of products such as pots or puppets are better made by specialists in childish and superfluous production. Communism will do well not to leave professions to enthusiasts. It will have the means, i.e. the time, to turn enthusiasts into professionals.

The division of labour, by now surely tried and tested, is not, as Marx claims ("The Poverty of Philosophy" II-2), to blame for differing talents. It is, however, the condition for their greatest possible development. Only where there is a division of labour is there space for differing talents to flourish, to flow from the mind into the world. Division of labour undoubtedly means freedom.

The scientific principle on which all hope for the future is based, is: Everyone can do something. Only factious drivel could possibly claim: Everyone can do everything. Thus, the author is not disposed to believe that with all this hype about creativity the future has begun. He has enough human labour on offer as things stand. What he demands is professional human labour, not something worse. The author would not even have the architect, who built the city in which he spends his life, push his cart.

Under the Media, the Muses Fall Silent

Foundations of a Science

The abolition of art succeeded in the historical period of intensified class struggle, which is called detente. Since time immemorial, the god of war was known as the enemy of the muses. Tübke still painted him that way. This is not true anymore. The enemy is no longer the god of war, now it is the goddess of peace. It is not Ares who cast out the muses, it is Eirene, the goddess of nuclear stalemate.

Detente is that state of the world where manufacturing death has crossed the threshold to abundance. All inequalities in the forces of destruction have disappeared behind the mutual ability to liquidate the human race, and since then no further explosive devices have been dropped or hurled through the air north of the Mediterranean. But detente is not peace; it is, at best, disarmament.

Once in a while, it may be possible to end a war without the victor fully grabbing the vanquished by the throat. But detente can only be clinched with a clear decision; one side has to triumph, the other perish. The epochal contradiction of world revolution and world counter-revolution is a fact. No-one can just turn it off. And so, world war takes place in this half of the century as a war of souls.

Spectral battles are fought. Between souls and no longer between bodies. Some souls are slaughtered; the rest are maimed and left to bleed. The aim of this war of souls is to undermine the opposing society before it undermines your own. In this war, the loser is the government whose people are the first to lose trust in what it says and stop heeding what it proposes. That's what it's all about.

In this new context of the war of souls, art at first received unusual and certainly excessive attention from governments. The beauty of art became a beauty appended to the art of persuasion, and the science of art became a strategic science. The ministries of culture were full of Clausewitzes. Art as such is something that governments are indifferent to, just as they are to philosophy or history as such. But now it was fully reforged: warforged.

Art would probably have survived this. Art can do a lot, why shouldn't it be able to kill?

But surprisingly, in the course of the detente there was another, unilateral disarmament measure by the East. It decided to stop making art and to start making non-art instead.

The Russians had a choice in the matter which the Americans did not have: they could put to use either art or non-art in the war of souls, and indeed they tried it with art for quite a while. The Americans didn't have a choice; for they had ceased to have art long ago. Apparently, however, when the Russians felt beleaguered beyond their limits and were forced to economise, this high technology became too extravagant for them. Art cannot just be procured cheaply from artists, any more than bombs from inventors. Both require a colossal environment. The quills in the Russian weapons registers proved to be particularly double-edged weapons.

The image is not really conducive to clarity. What does it mean? Art is a dangerous weapon, dangerous even for those who use it.

Art is the consciousness of a society, in art society has its for-itself and its willpower. Thanks to art, society is able to come to terms with itself, which steels its mettle. This includes, of course, the ability to question itself. A nation that has art has bitten the apple: it can say yes and no to itself.

Before a government allows the freedom to say no, it prefers to relinquish the yes, it thinks it can do without it. Governments do not necessarily wish to take delight in their people. It's enough if you don't have any trouble with them. The Russians ignored Stalin's suggestion that the superstructure itself sometimes had the effect of reacting back on the foundations of society. They stopped caring about the superstructure. An indifferent populace comes for so much less money than an approving one and, or so the Russians thought, it does the same service – at least for everyday purposes.

This explains why they followed the lead of the United States, and lined up with them to abandon art and crush it wherever it stirred. Not only were artists once again forbidden to shoot, they were suddenly forbidden even to take aim. In this, there is no difference now between the Russians and the North Americans. Their art is a thing of the past, their art-like things are interchangeable. The aspirations of socialism are now compatible with imperialism.

This is how art went missing on the planet in the last twenty or thirty years, and it was socialism that caused it to go missing. Whatever one may think of the reasons for this conciliatory impulse, the disadvantages are obvious. In the twentieth century, socialism has a natural intellectual hegemony, and any field of ideas in which it does not set the tone is out of sync with nature. One can hear the socialist voice missing, its silence is discordant. Moreover: The laws of war with physical weapons and those of war with weapons of the mind are not the same.

Nobody paid attention to the difference. Wars waged with physical weapons result in the most terrible devastation. Wars with mental weapons are devastating if not waged. There, war reduces human beings to rubble, here, peace reduces whatever is human to rubble.

Some friendly souls perceived the disappearance of art as a loss and a certain intractable sadness weighed upon their hearts. But most got used quickly to the new artless situation. What took the place of art wasn't no art at all, but what is here called non-art and by which is meant something meaningless, which is produced or used in ways that are vaguely reminiscent of those of works of art. If you hang a black square on the wall, what it has to do with a picture is that it hangs on a wall.

In the theory of signs, the idea arose that there could also be signs that signify nothing. In the past, one might have called them scribbles; but that, as was now proclaimed, would be seeing them too narrowly. Though the scribbles alluded to nothing, they were after all still allusions.

Non-art was able to present itself as art without a rupture.

Human beings can think and love it when their downfalls are accompanied by a theory. There is a theory of non-art, and this essay deals with it. The best way to explain a non-thing is to explain the thing: what the non-thing is not. The theory of art used to be called aesthetics.

Aesthetics is the science of art and at the same time its technique: both the description of its laws and the directions for its production. Art, as aesthetics tells us, is the following activity.

A subject (the artist, representing society in his own way) lays an object before the mind and heart of another subject (the audience, representing society in its own other way). The object can be a political story or just a painted peach. In both cases it is misperceived by the artist, and there is something of an intention in this incapacity for objectivity; in this way, the object ultimately also represents society and the object is also a subject, without ceasing to be an object. In the context of art, society negotiates with society about society.

(The meaning and purpose of the negotiation is the ideal, that is to say, the best way imaginable for the subject viz. humanity to come to terms with the object viz. the world. That only in passing).

The negotiation is always mediated by a vivid figuration, the work of art. The work of art imitates the object. It has three properties. It seeks to be similar to the object; it imitates the object by way of its stance towards the world, which is the real content of the work of art and the principle element in art, and thirdly, it does so skilfully: namely, in such a way that the public has the desire to enjoy it. It is a thing of delight. In order that it does not lack these properties, the imitation takes place in a commensurate time-tested form: a genre.

This is roughly and provisionally stated and it is not everything. Though as a rule of thumb, it suffices. No work of art functions differently. What kind of art human beings anticipated in the course of history, and particularly what kind they actually received, has often changed. All works of art also differ from one another. But all works of art are accounted for by aesthetics and fall under the above definition.

The word aesthetics is, to be precise, not a word in the plural. Aesthetics, as a branch of philosophy, is the theory of art, and there is only one theory of any particular thing.

In our times, however, – why actually our? – we encounter a phenomenon that has no right to appear: a deluge of (various) aesthetics. One no longer turns to aesthetics in the singular and instead revels in a whole plague of aesthetics in the plural. These have names like: production aesthetics, reception aesthetics, documentary aesthetics, material aesthetics, and so on and so forth. You can hardly understand any of these names. Anything to do with this gibberish can only be a house built on sand.

Anyone willing to try and find a meaning in the jumble of names could turn credulously to the new varieties of aesthetics for partial solutions. The weary brains of the 20th century, he might be trying to say, are not up to grasping the entirety of aesthetics, which is really not that easy. Short of breath as they are, they rather inflate its parts. Instead of conceptualising art as a whole, they expound on what the artist does, what the public does, what rights and duties the object is entitled to, and perhaps even what the work of art is. But the new varieties of aesthetics in the plural are not content with contributing to aesthetics in the singular. They are the ones who don't get along. They put on airs and act as if they themselves were somebody. But that doesn't work.

The new varieties of aesthetics are either included in aesthetics (and therefore superfluous) or not included, in which case they deal with something other than art.

The latter is what they do.

Production aesthetics is not something like the partial science of the processes by which works of art are created, but rather the theory that the work of producing art is itself the goal of art. The process of producing is supposed to be the product.

Reception aesthetics is not something like the partial science of the conditions under which the enjoyment of art takes place and the tricks with which artists make an impact, but rather the theory that art is always what any ordinary bystander makes of it. Stupid as it may sound, the difference between understanding and misunderstanding is denied and the consumer is urged to make use of the work of art without having first got the hang of it.

Object aesthetics is not something like the partial science of the suitability of materials for the arts, but rather the theory that the materials themselves are works of art. In documentary art, the object becomes irrelevant. It remains unprocessed, standing only for itself, and as object art it becomes the laughing stock of the cleaning ladies.

The aforementioned varieties of aesthetics isolate the three participants in society's discourse with society about society. Taken out of context, the artist, the audience and the artefact are helpless and one can twist them around. – Other varieties of aesthetics speak strangely about the work of art.

– The mediation of artistic discourse through the work of art is seen as a detour. Sidestepping this detour, artists are linked with the audience and encouraged to commune directly with their friends. This theory can perhaps be called picnic aesthetics. Those in the mood for something artsy should get together with others and do something nice.

– The main virtue of the work of art, the virtue of genres, is declared a sacrilege. This aversion is expressed in the various aesthetics of generic disorder: of the total non-artwork.

– Material aesthetics proclaims the right to steal from old works of art; it does so to challenge the immortality of the work of art. According to this theory, old works of art are works of a bygone age; they are obsolete and hence dead works of art, unless a contemporary artist takes pity and puts his signature on it. (If a child paints a moustache on the Mona Lisa, then that is not yet material aesthetics, or at most a trivial form. Material aesthetics is when Marcel Duchamp paints a moustache and declares that he is now on par with Leonardo, or above him).

However, the New Aesthetics in the plural are not as droll and harmless as they present themselves. Taken separately, they're all baloney. Together they are complete and consistent, and several little follies give rise to a big crime. The suggestion that this essay makes to the New Aesthetics is to dissolve their multiple forms and, though they are prudently never described as belonging together, to acknowledge themselves as the one aesthetics that they basically are: the aesthetics of non-art. For the founding of this aesthetics of non-art, a name is suggested: manipulation aesthetics.

Manipulation aesthetics double-deals the work of art out of the context of art and thereby dispenses with both the work of art and art without much effort.

Attempts were made for a while to comprehend the precepts of manipulation aesthetics by calling it formalism. This approach went deeper than was apparent at first glance, but ultimately it was not at all right and maybe even too honourable. What was right about the name formalism was that the creations of manipulation aesthetics have no content. As a result, it follows that they do not have any form either, and so it is better to drop the name.

Of course, there is some deceit in every art; its goal, apart from the true, the good, the beautiful, is always money and advertising. Parties, cliques and authorities pursue agendas and express themselves.

However, these pages wish to have understood under manipulation aesthetics much more and worse than the usual aesthetics of rewards and bribes with their modest manipulations. It is a comprehensive counter-aesthetics that is part of a comprehensive counter-consciousness. The 20th century only deceives on a large scale. The term manipulation aesthetics points to the ultimate, lethal manipulation. Manipulation aesthetics is a killer science: a science to do away with its subject. What it leaves behind is Snuff Art.[38]

How new is manipulation aesthetics?

In its conceptual form, it is old. Its basic ideas have been around for 200 years, though it is not at all aware of this. Since it denies the existence of a past, it is unaware of how inventive its own past has been.

But it had no hope of emerging in a real form until a few decades ago. Its aesthetic changelings could not appeal to anyone. What manipulation aesthetics brings forth is not intended for consumption and isn't consumed either. So, whatever it may have produced remained unknown. The works of non-art were left with the non-artists and did not reach the people.

Manipulation aesthetics could not have been saved from this intrinsic pickle even by the strong need that the New Thinking has for it, but for a timely and fortuitous technical occurrence that enabled the works it brought forth to exist without any consumers. This fortuitous occurrence was the invention of the media.

By the media is meant here broadcasting for hearing and seeing, and likewise see-newspapers.

The word media is, to be precise, not in the singular. It is the plural of medium. That the different media can be confused with each other is their strength; like beagle hounds, they always hunt in packs. Of course, they each answer to some dog names even if they're all after the same game. If, for example, news about cars is on the first page of a see-newspaper, it is 'Bild', if it is in the car section, it is 'Stern', but if you have to look for it under the heading 'Culture', it is 'Spiegel'. For those on the inside, the media are distinguishable by certain characteristics. But only those who speak of the media in general speak concretely.

Ever since the media were invented, non-artworks are actually

38 Snuff art or film depicts acts of violence (or violent sexual acts) as if taken directly from reality.

present as media artworks. The mode of being of media artworks is through the assertion of their existence by the media. They are not of this world, but of one in which rumours are taken at face value. The media say they exist; in this way they exist. They have taken the place of art, and this was accomplished without attracting much attention. The hustle and bustle around art is more than ever. Hardly anyone feels its absence.

Manipulation aesthetics thus has its Russian cause, the peace of renunciation in the aesthetic world war, and its American condition, the invention of the media. If somebody is overcome by a terrible nausea – knowing the cause may somewhat ease his discomfort.

THE H.M.

Attempt to Define the Media Man

Is it possible for someone to be an artist, and a world-famous one, without ever gratifying anyone with a work of art? What is marvellous about this question is that it at all arises. It is possible. It happens more and more.

It is possible if nobody knows the works of art and yet everyone has heard about the artist. It's the media that make this possible. The artists are fabulous guys; because the media call them that. And the planet applauds based on hearsay.

These kinds of artists belong to a human species not rooted in the ground of reality, but merely sprouted from that of the media. They are a form of Homo Mediarum, H.M. for short. Media persons are the media salvation teachers who don't teach any salvation. The media experts who are, at best, experts on media matters. The media statesmen who are pleasant to look at and otherwise have no influence in the state. Among all these are also the media artists who do not create any art.

A metaphor for heads that exist in the media world but not in the rest of the world, is the hero of the satellite TV series who goes by the name of Max Headroom.[39] His head isn't made of physical cells but of granulated grid dots. His face on screen is nothing but his true face, he doesn't have one anywhere else. His image is already his whole being. Max Headroom could also be called Max Kopfzimmer or Maxim Glawsalow; he inhabits the landscape of both western and eastern media.

Here, then, the West and the East are dealt with as one, something that has little hope of success when it comes to other subjects. But the world of the media is actually One World. In this, there is currently no difference.

From an economic point of view, the world of the media is the last remaining export article of the USA. Once upon a time, North American exports used to be considerable. They exported computers and duplicating machines, beauty lotions and washing powders. It is said that in the early days they even exported cars. Customers also owed to them the machines with which the messages of the media were received. Since then, however, they have stopped selling manufactured things.

Apart from grain – but what will they do the day the Russians come upon the idea of building some barns for themselves? … the only thing they can still dispose of, other than as a land of fodder suppliers, is the content of the media: the art of entertainment and the art of decline.

At one time, the technology of the media was American. Their function today is still American: doing away with the real world and replacing it with a media world, in which the media person cultivates his media audience, the inhabitants of the media world.

The media lie with real images and sounds. That they lie is well known and a platitude. Everyone knows the media lie, but everyone is determined not to believe what they know: they continue to go by the media as if they don't lie. The media often even readily

39 Fictional artificial intelligence character, advertised as "the first computer-generated TV presenter".

report that they lie and how they lie. This exercise is somewhat mischievous and wins hearts.

Like moths buzzing around a lamp in their random tracks, the truths, partial truths and inanities of the media buzz around reality in a disorderly for and against and submerge it in an indeterminate light. What is, ceases to be, when it is behind the veil of the media maya; things lose their material quality. Delusion is everywhere. Only a Buddhist can really understand the media.

But in truth it is not at all nothingness that is behind the facade. It is still the world which is kept hidden behind this facade. The fact is that the media have a content and serve a purpose.

All these mutually canceling reports, these truth-obscuring truths, and findings degraded to teasers, are intentionally false when taken en masse, and the totality of their movements is entirely controlled. A lot of commotion, and yet there is order behind it. There is a pattern beneath the chaos, as Einstein once said to Planck or someone else to someone else.

The pattern is the general message of the media. The general message of the media is the Big Lie.

The Big Lie implies that the state of society is immutable and this is how it should be.

This is such a mind-boggling sentence that it couldn't be said other than via the media. The Big Media Lie does not lie directly. It surfaces by erasing all desire for knowledge in the person to be deceived, by inducing an apathy towards knowledge and a general state of uncertainty. The media basically repeat the same lie that there is no such thing as knowledge. Anyone who tells you there is nothing to take exception to in society has convinced you that it is unexceptionable.

The approach is called maintaining balance.

Maintaining balance is the agreement that for every opinion, right or wrong, there has to be a counter-opinion. Mankind had assumed until now that a counter-opinion was only required for an incorrect or half-correct opinion and that all counter-opinions to the sentence "Human beings have two ears" were completely dispensable – from "Human beings have one ear" to "Human beings have innumerable ears". Now, maintaining balance admits of any number of ears, from one to infinity, including in fairness the number two among them.

The primary assertion of logic demands that of two mutually exclusive propositions only one or the other can be true. Maintaining balance would naturally allow this assertion of logic to have its say, as long as it is mixed with several contradictory assertions. It is based rather on ethics. It is considered impolite to want to know something exactly.

The mills of the media certainly grind the truth, but they grind it slowly. Every so often, when some dangerous information needs to be quickly fended off or any useful false information quickly pushed through, they resort to a crude intervention and launch a media campaign. In plain language: a media military campaign.

Then language control takes the place of maintaining balance. Then the media lie with one voice, and that doesn't work for them, that's not what has brought them so incredibly far. They do it reluctantly and only as an exception, only during prime time. And everyone is quite embarrassed to see them lying so openly. They seem then to be so honest.

Throughout the Middle Ages, the Christian church did not have such unchallenged dominion over souls as the media have today. Compared to the media, the church acted clumsily: it still lied. It may certainly be ingenious to swindle people with a great deal of effort. But the fine art of ingenuity lies in putting the idea out of their heads to inquire about the truth.

A country that has the media no longer needs censorship.

It had its origins, of course, in the United States, this wholesale delivery of zero news, for which the Russian word glasnost has meanwhile become prevalent. "Glasnost" could be rendered in plain language as "media truth". Someone who makes his judgments based on media truth is referred to as a "mature" or probably even "critical" citizen. – All media critics …

The media critics without exception … The media critics all and sundry and each and every one of them mislead their readers by blaming the technical inadequacies of the media for the Big Media Lie. They cannot help but admit that what the media reports is suspicious, and they propose that the messenger be beheaded. But if a messenger delivers something suspicious, it may be surmised that someone has given him something suspicious.

"Media" really stands for nothing other than "means". The more mundane word covers the sense of the foreign word. All means are somewhat damaging to whatever they carry out and have side effects: there are murky means and lame ones, those that are not too skillful and those that get into gear too slowly. But of all the ways of conveying facts, the moving image transmitted at the speed of a sunbeam is the fastest and clearest.

Whether the respective means is better or worse: as long as it conveys to the best of its ability, it can't be blamed for the message conveyed. The means does not sin. It does its work as intended by the owner: as a means to aid teaching, a means to stimulate the senses, a means to purge the body of toxic substances. Of course, any means can deliver the world if that is what its owner wants of it. The understanding of the word today is something like the following: The government means business: It has the means to force the people to swallow a bitter pill.

Only when one says that the means itself is the message does one give up asking what the message is and who it is from.

It is necessary to defend the media.

What's the point of the accusation that images replace concepts in the media – as if that weren't the intention? The parties in the USA display on their banners an elephant or a donkey or a governor or some other animal instead of an election promise.

What's the point of insinuating that the media wouldn't be able to deliver the information? They're not supposed to deliver it. In the media themselves there is neither any contradiction nor any inability. The media critics become media detractors when they attribute political depravity to the generic characteristics of the media. They accuse the media of being an inappropriate means of conveying the truth. The fact is that they are an appropriate means of conveying untruths. The error is quite crude.

The suspicion arises that media criticism is itself a medium and a way of making that, which is, evaporate.

If the media were understood as a service, one might as well have given up all hope. But they testify so agreeably to the ingenuity of our race when understood as a service of a secret service. Anyone who does not like to think little of humanity should understand them in this way. Humanism demands it. The decline in values partly stems, of course, from the way the world is going. In larger part, it is dictated.

With these remarks, the present essay finally comes to the subject of media arts.

A media artwork should not be understood as the distractions that the media itself creates in order to attract consumers. These are catchy things that evoke pleasure. They are just as sleazy or light-hearted as they are, and there is no need to lose any philosophical sleep about them. Media artworks, by contrast, are created outside of the media. They are works of non-art that artists devote themselves to for no other inducement than media coverage. (Indeed, by reporting about them, the media also create them).

The media arts have one advantage over the arts: their value can be measured. What's annoying about art is that you can't argue about it, or at least not with the prospect of victory; as regards the media arts, however, there isn't any need to argue about their quality. A piece of media art is as good as the coverage of it is extensive.

The value of media art is measured in space and time. It appears as the number of columns and the length of the broadcast. The media artworks are classified in the see-newspapers by means of a ruler and on television by the clock: by the time they take.

Though they are works of art without qualities, art finally becomes quantifiable with them. This quantifiability is somewhat restricted by the fluctuating value of broadcast time. Unused broadcast time (abstract broadcast time) also counts as broadcast time, but only of the lowest value. The colloquial term for broadcast time when no one is watching is "graveyard slot".

Cicero names the person who lets himself be guided by such "dubious means" (the media) as the *homo se dubium mediumque agens*. Two things can be inferred from this. The media existed even back then, and even then, it was considered sensible not to believe them. On the other hand: as long as it seemed strange if someone believed them, they did not exist in the modern sense.

The outdated media, by means of which our ancestors could learn about works of art, were the read-newspapers, accompanied at best by a few pamphlets and paperbacks. What was irksome to influencers was a medium that was in the possession of art lovers: the letters they wrote to each other. But all of them required a certain amount of attention; if you wanted to get to know their messages, you had to interpret them. And they neither had the monopoly on consumption nor the monopoly on taste with regard to the work of art.

These are the three shortcomings that have made the old media obsolete. The closer we look at the three shortcomings of the obsolete media, the more spectacular is the light thrown on the proficiency of today's media.

(1). The obsolete media could not be absorbed with far less effort than the works of art themselves.

The effort demanded of the book lover by a scholarly study and by the book it is about is not greatly different. Indeed, it takes longer to get the description of a picture into your head than it does to look at the picture. Before one reads the Hamburg Dramaturgy, one might just as well go to the theatre.

With this ineptitude of the obsolete media, one always had to reckon with those who knew the work. It was hardly possible to pass off works of quality as works of poor quality and vice-versa. The work coexisted with and disturbed the reports about it.

Media Law Number One is the Law of Acceptance. The medium must be easier to digest than the work of art it is about.

(2). The obsolete media allowed consumers some choice in the works of art they consumed.

Works of art can be produced and offered at little cost, and where consumption is not regulated, competition between the works is comparatively honest and comparatively free.

If the theatre of the Germans in the first half of the nineteenth century belonged almost exclusively to the following authors in succession: Kotzebue, Iffland, Raupach, Birch-Pfeiffer, this corresponded to the real wishes of the audience. Schiller's dramas were incredibly popular since his Christian-patriotic "Maid of Orleans" – popular for dramas of a poet. Compared to Kotzebue, however, his popularity could be ignored. There was hardly any dissimulation in all this. But if what regulated popularity at that time had already been the real media, the theatres would have performed neither Schiller nor Kotzebue. They would all have had to perform "Alarcos".[40]

Media Law Number Two is the Law of Sole Consumption. The medium can only classify works of art once it has the power to ensure that, if at all any works of art are taken note of in-house, they are, in any case, only those which it purveys.

(3). No matter how strange it may seem now, the obsolete media also used to refer to the judgment of art lovers while discussing the works of art. But the wholesale takeover of the work of applause only became possible after the media became both purveyors and arbiters of art rolled into one. What is enjoyed nowadays is not the work of art, but the report about the work of art.

In the old days, a director used to get drunk after a failed performance or voice suicidal thoughts in the lap of a prostitute. To-

40 Play by the romanticist Friedrich Schlegel, which Hacks dismissed as "nonsense".

day, he happily rushes to his television set and listens to the news of how intolerable and exceedingly significant he is. Since the work of art can now be quantified, a widely broadcast flop is a victory. The boos of the mere earthly world are reconfigured, even as the report dwells on them, as media bravos. For all intents and purposes, they are preferred to the mere earthly bravos. Boos prolong the enjoyment of the report.

Media Law Number Three is the Law of Sole Judgment. Taste can only be fully subjugated to a taste regime if judgments of taste are made solely by granting or refusing media space.

So much about the media as the sole reporters, sole consumers and sole judges of works of art. So much about how they finished off art and replaced it with another commodity under the old brand name of art. This commodity guaranteed that there was no scarcity in the stores; supplies have probably only increased.

But even a monopoly sells a commodity that people can use more easily than one that they cannot use. As such, the circulation of art is wholly in the hands of those who own the media. The works of non-art are the only ones available, and they are sold without a hitch. The media never stand still. There's always something on TV. The public does not resist the media interpretation of a media artwork. – Indeed, the public prefers an interview with the media artist rather than any interpretation of a media artwork. For the hobby of man is man.

The media artist is the H.M. who produces the media artworks. He does this in the same reality, in which other people also pursue their business and their pleasures; he too exists in this reality in a way. Somehow or other the H.M. does also live in the world. But the world is his secondary residence.

We are talking about prominent figures of the century, lionised celebrities, looming larger than life. Quite a few people believe that the H.M. works his fingers to the bone in his studio though his life is filled with pomp and splendour. It's the other way around. The H.M. is idle only as an artist. As an artist, he is lazy and overproductive; he produces a lot in quantitative terms, albeit in keeping with his own indolent ruminations. As a human being, by contrast, he is busy as a beaver.

He then lives the life of a full-time member of the jet set. His entire personal life is a professional life: a life as a subject of media reportage. Reporters always have their eye on high society, and the H.M. will seek out and partake of high society, and not avoid it.

He also cultivates picture-perfect acquaintances. He associates with presidents and those sentenced to death. He is often seen with boxers.

He frequents all the artists' watering holes. Not because of the artists there, but because of the reporters.

He is at all gatherings. Hardly any gathering is so unimportant and far-flung that the H.M. does not take part in it; he positions himself in the space captured by the angle of a camera and lingers there. Everyone is happy to see him there again, but who thinks about the hardships he had to endure to get there? He follows the cameras; he does not rest. He can sleep while standing. He can sleep while listening. He can sleep while talking. He still has his best snooze on night flights. The H.M.'s everyday life, other than while making art, is backbreaking work.

And yet his life of creative endeavour is only the condition for his actual endeavour: showcasing himself.

Human beings are social beings. All human beings exist by virtue of their being and also by virtue of their being observed. Both ways of being work back and forth, who can separate them neatly? Even real artists were (and are) expected to introduce themselves to their fellow human beings. Some do. Others don't.

The German novelists of the twentieth century, for example, were absolutely dissimilar in the matter. Thomas Mann counted it among his duties to occasionally leave the desk which was his abode, present himself to his readers and suffer having pictures taken of himself. Arno Schmidt, on the contrary, refused this service to the public, so he had no public. He had the choice between the media world and the Lüneburg Heath,[41] and he made his choice. There are no grounds for any moral considerations on this point. What in hell should a novelist do on a screen?

What makes the difference is the following. Is the photo the photo of the body, or is the body the body to the photo?

But even this distinction, sharp as it is, allows for crossovers. The moment a poet falls in line when a photographer asks him to stare into a river surrounded by bushes, or stroll down a rain-soaked street, or stroke his cat in the window of his room, he has already lost some of his sense of decency and moved closer to the H.M. He already seems to be an actor playing himself. He behaves as the lens wants to see him; a pictorial artist moves the poet's exterior, and a spontaneous feeling moves his interior. The step from the staged media novice to the media artist would be complete if he leapt into the water into which he is staring.

What the art of media representation demands of the H.M is no small thing. He has to disguise himself; he has to set himself up against absurd backgrounds and allow himself to be steered into movements contrary to nature. He's at the top of the ranking ladder, he has achieved that goal. But he doesn't stop paying the price for a minute. Every editorial trainee is his superior. Every production assistant is his sergeant and drills him. As the soul of the swift Achilles said to Odysseus, when the latter once visited Hades, he would rather be the slave of a nobody on earth than king of the shadows. The H.M. is both the one as well as the other. He is the slave of a nobody on earth and also king of the shadows.

In his work of self-display, he has to follow the generic laws of self-display. He doesn't simply put himself on display. He does so in a media-friendly manner. Although no one wants to get acquainted with his works of art – everyone must want to get acquainted with him.

The easiest way to practice media-friendly behaviour is to

41 From 1958 until his death in 1979, Arno Schmidt lived in self-imposed isolation in the small village of Bargfeld in the Lüneburg Heath.

show off an optical trademark. An optical trademark is a badge by which the H.M. can be identified as someone special and imprinted in memory. Such as the Beuys hat. Or the Warhol wig. Wagner with his beret was also a man of the future in the matter of trademarks. Rarely will it be the face by which one recognises the media person. When the media consumer exclaims: That's the one who always kisses the airfields, he's famous, I've seen him quite often! then he is on the right path. After the third airfield, the H.M. has made it. He then belongs to television like the man who presents the weather forecast.

What is media-friendly is a catchy name: one that is catchy across language barriers. East and West now speak the same language in the media, too bad for the Russians that the language is English. English has a double advantage when it comes to the names of media persons. For one it is the undisputed world language, and then it's also shorter. The name Robert Wilson is easier to remember than the name Konstantin Lopushansky.

It is good for the image-devouring media if the H.M. has a wealth of imperfections and can put them on view. He works, as he shows, in various arts; these can be by all means unprofitable, as long as they are imageable. In the many things he dabbles in, he appears as a man of all-round imageability. In addition to the special genre below, which he does not master, he is also expected not to master some other genres.

The H.M. gains his artistic fame through media-friendly behaviour. Everything would be finally in place if it weren't necessary for him to also pronounce his presence in words while putting himself on view.

The media are called audiovisual and this is how they are. The pictures on television are accompanied by something spoken, the pictures in the see-newspapers are accompanied by something written. There has to be a text for each picture. How else would the viewer find out what he is supposed to be seeing in the picture? – Now, the text that the H.M. attaches to the picture of himself is threatening, like sailing through rough seas, and in whatever trivial things the H.M. trots out, there is also a certain mastery.

Artistic fame, once won, cannot be lost. There are old men who happily walk around in the splendour of their youthful fame without having added a single title to it in the course of their lives. There is, however, one exception to the rule that artistic fame cannot be lost. A careless word can shatter overnight the most well-established fame and for all times. In particular, when the H.M. speaks, he is not allowed to say anything unexpected, i.e. he is never allowed to think.

What does he talk about? He talks about his art and for that matter everything else.

Manipulation aesthetics requires him to present quite complicated things about his art, but at a low level of unintelligibility and without technical terms from the subject. When he talks nonsense, it is commonplace nonsense: pop nonsense, folk idiocies. A loner speaks out in front of millions, that's the task before him, and he does this by means of a tone developed for this purpose, a mix of subculture babble and ponderous obfuscation. – An individual interview of a media artist by a media professional might proceed as follows.

A H.M. inscribed his signature on a brick and put it on display with the title "Grazing Rock Rabbit" With much critical energy, the magazine editor raises the question of the inadequate similarity of the piece with the natural object that it represents. Then the H.M. will reply:

I find it similar.

Or:

You know, I don't understand any of that myself.

It is this kind of utterance that builds confidence these days.

Rather than appearing alert, the H.M. gives the impression of falling asleep during the interview.

But among the media persons there are also those – so that nothing is left unconsidered – who present what is stupid with a semblance of intelligence. They emit sparks like sparklers. (A sparkler is a device that is a part of Christmas accessories. Its sparks do not ignite. It sparkles away in cosy comfort).

When the media artist talks about how things are related to each other, this is usually done in group discussions. He joins other media persons from other areas of production to answer questions, about which he understands just as little as he does about art. Life poses the questions, the talk show disposes of them.

The platitudes of the H.M.: Human beings are wicked. The world is bloody. Most things are doubtful. He gets along pretty well with these three sentences. They bring forth familiar sounds, as if homespun. Anyone who listens (but no one does) will find that the H.M. absolutely refrains from any meddling in affairs of state. He practices "abstinence in political judgments", like Schiller's 'Horen'.[42]

Furthermore, and finally: the H.M. is always asexual.

Even when it comes to the flesh and its inclinations, the H.M. has an effacing effect. A soda-like aura floats around him. His appearance is characterised by a man-on-the-street indistinction and impotence. He is neither thoughtful nor attractive. He is seldom well-built, usually emasculated, and the Countess Tolstoy gives quite a good description of his breed when she describes a "darkling" – the name with which the members of the house of Tolstoy referred to their own kind when amongst themselves:

"He's stubbornly silent, has a straight face, very dark hair, blue glasses and is blind in one eye. From his few words one cannot get any idea of his views!"

This is the stuff that dream persons are made of. Headroom too stutters.

The planet people see in the media is different from the one they inhabit. Art gives a picture of the world. In media art, the

42 German literary journal published by Schiller from 1795 to 1797; it was the cornerstone of German Classicism, represented among others by Goethe and Schiller.

media world offers a self-portrait. Many think of media consciousness as a form of false consciousness – but that's a venerable term from the contemplative and educated old days. Media consciousness is the waking state of unconsciousness in regard to people's knowledge of themselves and the powers that govern them.

The arts flourish in the media. In reality, the arts no longer exist. Artists show themselves in droves in the media. In reality, the art lover can wander around with his lamp for a long time and will not find one. In a way, media persons are more believable than normal persons who naturally do not walk around as their own documentation.

But those who are still willing to make a distinction between what is and what is claimed, will hold fast to the knowledge that media persons are invented by an apparatus of creators.

The poet, said the ancients, is born. The media poet is made. Not only are his works of art created by the media, he himself is a creation of the manipulation department. He is really nothing better than a fabricated creature.

If it turns out that he becomes a nuisance, your position is awkward. You have the right, but hardly the power, to turn him off. It is best to discuss the matter with his manager.

[Left-Wing Art]

Left-wing art is such art as is created by Marxist-Leninist artists, people of education and genius. It emulates reality, particularly regarding concepts of time and the existence of causal relationships in society. It is characterised by truth, beauty and virtue. It enjoys popularity among the working masses.

Left-wing art is also known as Socialist Realism. It is cheerful, furthers anti-imperialist revolution, and afterwards, it earns the Stalin Prize.

Stories and Poems

[not later than 1947]

[Two Heavenly Tales]

At the time when the great temple was being built in Nebria, the master carpenter Borromeo fell from the roof of the building in the midst of the devotees who were about to consecrate the temple, and they all cried "holy, holy" because they were unaware that he had slipped on an olive pit and thought he had come straight down from heaven. Ever since that time St. Borromeo performed many more miracles, but when he appears in images with a wooden implement, it is mistakenly thought to be a cross. It's just the roof beam that had been ripped out.

Saint Boniface fell so much in love with a beautiful daughter of the highly erotic region of Cucumbria that he did not want to let go of her, although of course he was supposed to live in celibacy; and the LORD was very angry at this and threatened him with eternal damnation. Then Saint Boniface said: "If you condemn me now, you will be rid of me forever, and it will be your loss, but if you let me go ahead, it will all be over in two weeks."

Ameli and the Frog Prince

There was a little girl whose name was Ameli and, as you will see, she was nobody's fool. Once she went walking across the land in order to do something for her health, and she came to a park with fountains and swans and aster beds and such extraordinary things. There was a high iron fence around the park, and when Ameli wanted to go in, the doorkeeper suddenly stuck his head out of the window. He was wearing a red uniform and a long pointed cap. "Are you even invited?" he grunted. "Of course," said Ameli. And that was indeed very quick-witted.

In the interior of the park, there was a castle, and in front of it was a pond, and next to it shone a golden throne, and on it sat a big, green frog with a golden crown on its head, and anyone who had the slightest idea about the matter could see that this was the frog prince. The ministers stood all around. They were fat and wore frock coats and long pointed caps. "It is your duty, Majesty," they kept on saying, "the state demands it."

"What's the matter?" Ameli asked the Prime Minister. "He won't tell us how to charm him back," he whispered. "He wants to stay a frog."

"I want to remain a frog," said the frog prince; "I would rather sink in a swamp than in morals: I like my green color very much, it calms the eyes (which is why they even make green boards in schools lately). And the frogs are very agreeable subjects, they don't go to court, they don't wage wars, and they sing so beautifully when the moon is shining at night."

Ameli looked pityingly at the Prime Minister. "Have you all never read Grimm's fairy tales?" She ran to the throne and kissed the frog king square on the mouth. Hey presto! The most handsome prince stood there and said: "Alas, now the horrid business of ruling has to begin again. Well then, so be it." He married little

Ameli, and they lived and ruled together, and since there isn't a word of truth in the story anyway, nothing else changed in the state.

The Man from Sing-Sing[43]

This is a story told to me by the dean of the philosophy department at Columbia College. It proves, as the philosopher said, the relativity of the terms "good man" and "bad man", or at least the difficulty of properly distinguishing them right away from one another. I will tell it in my own words.

The Dean was driving late at night on one of America's major highways. He was in a good mood: in about two days he would be home enjoying the celebration of his fiftieth anniversary in office. He saw a man standing by the road and waving to him, so he picked him up. The man didn't look unusual. What was unusual was that he was unable to specify a destination. And really unusual (at least the Dean had never experienced anything like it) was that when asked where he was from, he candidly replied: Sing-Sing. In fact, the man perched on the foam-padded car seat next to the dean was one of the most renowned pickpockets and auto thieves of the States. This is how he was spending his first night in freedom in ten years. The dean was in the habit of teaching that one should think the best of strangers as a matter of principle. But the circumstances made him forget this principle. He drove through the ever so dark night with nervous haste. And thinking that at high speed the thief would not be able to attack him without endangering himself, he let the speedometer arrow rise to horrendous heights. Then a police officer stopped him for speeding. The dean got out, and his guest too took the opportunity to stretch his legs a little. The dean showed his papers, and it turned out that here was a cop who didn't like academics. Now American police officers have the power and ambition to invent strange punishments. The one we are talking about managed to discover that an unimportant certificate was missing, and he ordered the dean, under threat of a heavy fine, to fetch this certificate and present it at the same place within

43 Maximum-security prison in New York.

three days. In three days, that meant: the dean had to drive to the college in great haste, take the paper out of the drawer there and return again without delay in three and a half days, while missing out on the feast in his honour – in order to satisfy the democratic institution of authority. There was little to be done. And though he was in the habit of teaching the entirely opposite course of action, the dean flew into a rage and, as they drove on, berated his unsolicited fellow passenger with unkind words. But the man from Sing-Sing retained the mild temper he had continually shown. Instead of going on grumbling, he pulled a small piece of crumpled paper out of his coat pocket and stuck it on the windshield in front of the dean's eyes. It was the carbon copy of the warrant from the cop's notebook, which he had stolen without any effort.

The Wench Factory of Tahoua

Tangier, January 12, 1954. – For two weeks there's been talk between Senegal and Egyptian Sudan of a highly unusual business venture which had just been brought to an end for the time being by the police authorities in Tahoua, French West Africa. The black banana pickers in Dakar had to clutch their big bellies in laughter, and the brown cotton pickers in Omdurman nearly fell into the Nile with glee. And only a couple of filthy rich sheikhs and pashas are not quite so happy about the wench factory that two foreign legion deserters had been running in a village near Tahoua for more than two years.

It all started in 1951. The Czech Miros Čap and the Dutchman Jan van Ziebourg had escaped from the legion. They were in the heart of one of the most inhospitable areas in Africa. And they could not dare to be seen in the civilised world – not before they had earned the fortune that is required to outwit the law in Europe as well. But how to start? Well, there are only two ways to make a fortune in those parts. One is to own plantations that are as extensive as possible. The other: trafficking in young women. Jan and Miros didn't own any plantations, so they had to trade in women. Their knowledge of the Arabic languages and customs, which as men of talent they had quickly acquired, came to their aid.

They supplied women servants, women slaves and harem women to the courts of the small native potentates. Business went well. But it didn't yield the dividends expected by the two entrepreneurs, who of course had considerable expenses of their own. They failed to establish any international connections. And their 'goods', which they 'bought' partly in coffee houses and partly from native fathers in rags, were not of particularly good quality.

Once this became evident, Jan and Miros sat down in front of a row of whiskey bottles and pondered the basics of economics. And after a while, Jan, the more thorough of the two, had a great idea. “The producers of raw materials always earn the least,” he said to Miros. What do we give such a father for his daughter? A bottle of schnapps, or 100 to 250 frs (that’s 1.10 DM to 2.75 DM in German money). “We do the trading and earn our share, fine. But who do you think always makes the most money?” – “Who?” asked Miros. “I’ll tell you,” said Jan triumphantly: “the processing industry.”

From that time on the girls were no longer sold as God had created them. They were born again, so to speak, in Jan and Miro’s wench factory. The crafty entrepreneurs cleaned up their goods “for sale” with the most fancy cosmetic remedies. They painted the skin of the black girls an enticing almond brown, they painted their teeth white and their lips pale pink. They spruced up their hair to fall in strands instead of crinkling up in curls, and they fed their victims tantalizing chemicals that made them appear perky and appealing.

These remedies did not last long. After a few days, the colors faded, the hair took on its natural form and the eyes lost their radiance. But those few days were enough to sell the girls at a tremendous profit in this country where women are scarce. Complaints were not accepted. The cheated buyers couldn’t defend themselves: in North Africa, the trade in women is as illegal as it is common. And the clientele was large enough.

This remarkable factory could have continued to produce the most exquisite beauties for a long time if Jan van Ziebourg had not met a girl one day in a tavern in Tahoua, who enraptured him beyond description. Her name was Dina. The owner of the tavern was her father. Jan wanted to buy her from him. But the old man turned down all offers without appearing to be the least offended. “If you marry her, you get her,” he said. Women are scarce in this country. And Jan, who had a longing once again for a really beautiful girl, married Dina.

Within a week, Dina lost her classy nostrils, most of her teeth, and a few other charms that cannot be described more closely.

She didn't exactly become ugly, but she was no longer the dazzling beauty whom Jan had married. Jan waited for Miros, who was on a business trip at the time. Miros came back and acted innocent. Then there was a fight. Jan was the stronger, and it turned out that one of the duped buyers, the Sheikh of Tidjikja, had bribed Miros to fabricate Dina secretly. The Sheikh's revenge had succeeded. Jan had been taken in by his own swindle.

Unfortunately, Jan wasn't businessman enough to take that hit. He lost his nerve, ran to Tahoua to the French registrar of marriages and sued for divorce. This is how the whole story became official. The police confiscated the wench factory.

The Royal Court Moves House

The king lived in his royal palace, which was built on a high mountain. The mountain was densely forested, and when autumn dyed the crowns of the trees with colour, the mountain lay with the forest and the castle most charmingly in the sun. This is where the subjects brought their taxes once a year.

The taxes always amounted to a tenth of what each subject had harvested. The cabbage farmer brought three cabbages, the chicken farmer brought six eggs. The way up to the castle was steep, and nobody you or I know likes to give anything away. But they could spare the tenth if they had to, and it had also always been like that. All in all, it can be said that the king got on tolerably well with his subjects.

One day while he was out walking, the tobacco tin fell out of the king's hand. An old country woman sprang up, picked up the can and gave it to the king.

The king gave her a silver penny for the trouble, and the old woman said:

"Oh, Mr. King, I wish we could meet every day."

When the walk was over, the king said to his entourage in astonishment: "My people wish to see me more often, who would have thought it?" He became really enthusiastic. He made up his mind that henceforth he wanted to live with his subjects. And without delay the herald set off on his rounds and announced:

"The king is moving into the city!"

The jubilation that arose wasn't small.

All the carts that the country had were now needed for the move. This created a certain shortage in the market and not all of the harvest could be brought in. But finally, the king's furniture and suitcases of clothes and boxes of porcelain arrived undamaged at the riflemen's clubhouse. It was there that the king had taken up residence. He had to live somewhere after all.

His chamberlains and valets had to live somewhere too. All houses that had a solid roof were cleared for the royal court. Of course, the king's retinue also had its own retinue, it's really amazing how many children such a valet can have.

The streets were renamed and given names befitting the court. Dyers Street, Tanners Street and Fish Market now became Lord Street, Knight Street and Dragoon Market. The streets were now also used as coach routes. Passage was closed to fruit carts, pedestrians and donkeys.

The king liked being among his people, although some noises disturbed the peace to which he had become accustomed in the forest. The blacksmith's hammers hammered too loudly, and the cheering and singing in the beer garden was too noisy. That was put an end to and the beer garden and the smithy were closed down.

The beer garden owner and the smith were irked by this. These two men formed a party demanding the king's return to his castle. It was called the Castle Party.

The king released animals that could be hunted into the citizens' gardens, especially hares, rabbits and partridges. Incidentally, he called the virgins of the city together and conducted a ballet with them.

The Castle Party gained popularity.

The king was forced to set up an opposing party, the City Party, which stood for the court remaining in the city. Its chairman was the confectioner. Seeing that the children of the valet eat a lot of sweets.

Now the king had two daughters, Ilse-Marie and Ermensinde.

For years, Ilse-Marie had been acquainted with a troll, with whom she used to meet in the forest as soon as it got dark. Ermensinde, on the other hand, had a habit of climbing out of the window in her sleep and wandering through the meadows in her nightgown, especially on nights when the moon was shining.

That hadn't bothered anyone up on the mountain. Since they were living in the city, however, the king's daughters did not go unnoticed. There were always people who met the princesses. And each time Ilse-Marie visited her troll or Ermensinde moon-wandered, it was in the newspaper the next morning.

Ermensinde's nightgown was transparent, and the moon now revealed that she had crooked legs.

The princesses longed to return to the castle and therefore secretly funded the Castle Party.

The king, who secretly funded the City Party, wondered where the Castle Party got all that money from. But things were as they were. Both parties were equally rich and equally powerful.

Such a situation tears a people apart. It looked almost like civil war and people were starting to get worried. Should the king stay in the city or go back to the castle mountain? The question became a matter of concern for everyone – until the day when someone found the solution and said:

"It's probably best to have no king at all."

From that hour the country was no longer a kingdom. The royal family was stripped of its nobility and was forced to go abroad. The king spent the years of his banishment attending all meetings of kings, at which he always made the same speech.

"Colleague Majesties", he said in an imploring tone, "stay where you are, under no circumstances move to the city. Believe me, it would be the biggest mistake you can make."

Frau Thousand-feet Must Wash Today

Frau Thousand-feet must wash today,
A thousand socks precisely.
Upon a rowan leaf a spray
Of wind that dries them nicely.
A thousand socks is quite a lot.
A thousand socks a game is not.
A thousand greetings, all repeat,
A busy day, Frau Thousand-feet?

To hang them out a cobweb thin,
Pine needles keep them tethered,
A shepherd's purse to bring them in,
Two hollow nuts as cupboard.
A thousand socks, gosh, that's tough,
A thousand socks is quite enough.
A thousand greetings, all repeat,
A busy day, Frau Thousand-feet!

[1964, first version 1949]

Errors

A cat that was a rosy red,
A mouse that was sky blue,
At Anton square is where they met
And saw each other true.

The mouse looked for a place to hide
But then: No need, it said.
With licking lips I never spied
A cat that's rosy red.

The cat crept up in expectation,
Tongue and teeth astir,
Until it saw the strange complexion
Of its luncheon's fur.

The cat then let the mouse go free
Again due to the hue,
And it said: How can there be
A mouse that is sky blue.

They wandered freely off with that,
Each one to its own house,
Right, to Weissensee, the cat,
Left, to Lichtenberg, the mouse.

Ladislaus and Komkarlinchen

Once there was a soldier,
The soldier had a mouse,
Her name was Komkarlinchen,
The soldier's Ladislaus.

The soldier loved the fighting,
The spoils and fame to score,
But his dear Komkarlinchen,
He loved her even more.

She ate the bread that he ate,
And in his beard did bed,
Her dwelling was his pocket
While bound for wars ahead.

But when he went to battle,
The soldier with his pet,
She jumped out of his mantle
And like the wind she fled.

Then overcome with worry,
He ran in hot pursuit,
Criss-crossing through the army
Of Roman troops afoot.

And since she ran just rearwards
And never to the front,
The battle did without him
As it was lost or won.

The war grew ever older,
The war turned thirty year,
Older than some soldier
In life could persevere.

And those who loved the fighting
Saw spoils and fame with glee,
At sea lay dead and buried
Or else in Saxony.

But from all ill winds blowing
Came out without a grouse
Thanks to his Komkarlinchen
The soldier Ladislaus.

News of the Life of the Peramblers

Down garden paths in Asian land,
trail off to the perambler.
They have tusks as white as sand,
their ears could not be ampler.

From Tokyo to Athens is found
not one in best of weather.
They only ramble all around
upon a yellow heather.

On the yellow grass, indeed,
they've been growing roses.
They sniffle lavendery weed
and pluck it with their noses.

No famine ever raised its head,
and they can't cook moreover:
who needs dinner, when you're fed,
with sniffling done and over.

If ever it starts raining there,
while at a fair or gala,
they lift the left ear in the air
instead of an umbrella.

And if a winter harsh does fall,
with icy roads and rivers,
they wrap the right ear, not a shawl,
around to beat the shivers.

And so without a want or woe,
no sparring and no scrambling,
quite rid of every care they go
perambling, no: just rambling.

A doctor of high scholarship
once landed there so keenly.
They wished him well, a pleasant trip,
and waved their ears serenely.

[not later than 1957]

October Song

The proles had had it up to here
For the peasants it couldn't have come faster
They put Kerensky out on his ear
The past they put out to pasture
    It happened in October
    That such a sight was seen
    In Russia's Petrograd
    In 1917

The soldier did his rifle turn,
A prole he was once more
The generals were forced to learn
Who really fights the wars
    It happened in October
    That such a sight was seen
    In Russia's Petrograd
    In 1917

On an empty belly the muzhik read
An order by decree
That he who now shall eat the bread
Is he that tills the field
    It happened in October
    That such a sight was seen
    In Russia's Petrograd
    In 1917

Through monocles the gents did see
Their rule it was ill-fated
And ere a sailor in the Neva did pee
The gents were expropriated

It happened in October
That such a sight was seen
In Russia's Petrograd
In 1917

And he who sings this song to you
He lives in a new world
The prole, the muzhik, red soldiers too
Have all this place unfurled
It happened in October
That such a sight was seen
In Russia's Petrograd
In 1917

Strike Song

They own all machines, the bosses
from your work their pockets line.
While their profits are your losses,
how'll your fortunes ever shine.
Man of work, get up and fight,
And be conscious of your might,
All the wheels grind to a still,
If your mighty arm it will.

They mince words so smooth and chummy,
full of talk of partnership.
And the cakes they gorge so yummy,
leave you just a soup to sip.
Man of work, get up and fight,
And be conscious of your might,
All the wheels grind to a still,
If your mighty arm it will.

And they maim and murder millions,
if by profit they are told.
But beware their nuclear canons,
they are aimed to keep you cold.
Man of work, get up and fight,
And be conscious of your might,
All the wheels grind to a still,
If your mighty arm it will.

So ask yourself for whom you sweat,
is it for them, is it for me?
Is it your class that gets ahead,
or is it the bourgeoisie?

Break the double yoke, be free,
break the need of slavery.
Break the slavery of need,
bread is freedom, freedom's seed.

Turn off the power, douse the furnace,
leave the factory, shut the doors.
Now it's time to fight in earnest,
Onward for the people's cause.
Man of work, get up and fight,
And be conscious of your might,
All the wheels grind to a still,
If your mighty arm it will.

[1962]

Lumumba's Death

At Congo stands a big tree red.
Patrice Lumumba, the hero, is dead.

Lumumba lies with bloodsoaked chest,
Because he had trust, when to fight was best.

The king spoke of freedom, always lying,
While his army was toward midday flying.

Lumumba spoke: Let's avoid war,
It's dying soldiers I'm sorry for.

He called for friends from overseas,
For they should have been keeping peace.

They held his mouth closed shut.
And that was all the peace they got.

Lumumba through the jungle fled,
Okito and M'Polo with him led.

In the jungle they were caught,
As the king his wedding sought.

But when Lumumba was in prison bout,
the people asked to seek him out.

For forty thousands pounds in silver bullion
they sold him to the mining union.

Are you ready yet to die?
I am not ready to die.

There they shot him through his chest,
because he had trust, when to fight was best.

> Patrice Lumumba, Prime Minister of the Republic of Congo, was murdered by the General Secretary of the United Nations, Dag Hammarskjöld, on or before 12.2.1961. The "Blue Helmets" were the Foreign Legion of the USA back then already. Lumumba was replaced by Colonel Joseph Désiré Mobutu.[44]

44 Original annotation by Peter Hacks.

[not later than 1971]

You Shall Deny Me Nothing

You shall deny me nothing,
I want the last remains,
If pleasure yet be mounting,
A villain who refrains.
Our bliss will calm our waning,
Let death have naught remaining
But hoses limp from draining
And bare-licked splintered panes.

The father of our pleasures,
That grim old man of bone,
Adds to all closing measures
At last his very own.
The puffballs and the planets,
The fate of all the poets. . .
Us to the dark he plummets,
My love, and then alone?

So in the world's hands trusting,
The thousands keeping pace,
You shall deny me nothing,
Each other let's embrace.
Till languidly contented,
We on our own relented,
Our feet in each cemented
To silently retrace.

1. 8. 1973

Ulbricht sadly has passed, so too the days of statecraft in
Germany.
To Goethe am I drawn ever more and deeper.
Oh dear friend, take not your heart back now. Lest naught else
remain
But to inculcate the art of a barbaric time.

[not later than 1974]

Ask Not Whether Love is Worth It

Ask not whether love is worth it,
Ask whatever, but not that.
End that does the start inhabit,
Dyes the middle pale and flat.

Ask not what will be tomorrow,
Keep us strong and undeterred.
In joy rejoice and feel no sorrow
For the sadness afterward.

Life's designs exploring yonder,
Surging to unfold their plot,
Should I, shan't I? – if you ponder,
In that case you'd better not.

For the bud becomes a coffin,
If you winter dread in May,
Circumspection beckons ruin,
Which it wants to keep at bay.

[between 1974 and 1988]

Asides

The Party
One can live with the party. My wish, were I to have a right,
would be, that it be a little more partisan.

Whimsical
Freedom of the press, well. But demanding truth of the press,
If I am right, no-one has dared to do before.

Democratic Press
Thieves and liars here too, so the pamphlet tells me.
No journalists though. There's none of that lot at least.

CIA
Find out what God costs. Surely he can be blackmailed.
We have Woytila already, it's time the old man played dice.

[1988]

Trying Times

Lenin's roaring red October
Nudged humanity to rise,
Well, it got us somewhat closer
To the gates of paradise.
Trying times, long way to go,
Some things, I find, are far too slow.

Nodding robots with the know-how
Do all work of hand sans wage.
Pills teach women how to fuck now.
Where, o where's the golden age?
Trying times, long way to go,
Some things, I find, are far too slow.

A fool is printed, I'm forbidden.
What on earth won't you permit,
Pegasus, my winged stallion,
My red comrade, fighting fit?
If with humour you've been blessed,
Life seems quaint, quite queer at best.

A sun bereft of colour shining
Seeks behind the clouds its lot.
You too, dearest, leave me pining,
You're somewhere else, where I am not.
Trying times, long way to go,
Some things, I find, are far too slow.

The Little Unicorns

I
What is beautiful about nature: that it isn't like Berlin.

II
Were it more like life, art would hardly be cheerful.

III
But the little unicorns, as if they were nothing but eyes,
Big and round. Their horn, in sterner old age so disdainfully
  killing,
is yet soft with down, their not-of-this
world-being
Less sturdy than then and less robust their chastity.
Their innocence still trusting. Should you then come across a
  little
Unicorn in the forest, you must take care to only touch it
  by hand,
If you want to take it along and care for it true-hearted.
For if you just touch it and walk on thereafter,
  it will die.

[1988]

Make Haste, O You Hours

Make haste, o you hours, my dearest is coming.
Why dawdle, why dither, what's keeping you, pray?
And down with you, sun, be done with your shining.
You day, don't you get it, no longer need stay.

With honking and screeching, the din ever growing,
Life has become such a yoke, what the hell.
Away with all business. O hours, get going.
And if you were seconds, I'd hate you as well.

I cannot but wait for that gaze all aquiver,
Those luminous eyes, o so tender, to see.
Begone with you, hours, it's best if forever.
My dearest is nigh, let the world cease to be.

Couplets

Shaw
Shaw liked it well when to Stalin he came.
For 50 years, he's been out of the game.

Imperialism, a vampire
The beast is dead. Dead, and I stress
It may suck blood, it's dead nonetheless.

Wonder of the battle in Congo
The Yanks have Kabila surrounded,
Who do they run into? Lumumba's spirit.

Monster of the Century
Who of them siphoned the most blood off?
Was it Churchill, Hitler or Gorbachev?

FRG
Who thinks to fear this land he needn't bother
With eyes blindfolded goes into the slaughter.

Surveillance State
This land, for which my own I had to barter,
Hears not my woes. Eavesdropping is its charter.

Organised crime
Criminality when widely prevalent
Is also often called the government.

Voting Day
It's time to vote, so I raise my voice,
I vote for capital, I have no choice.

Crash
The market economy, the Federal Bank makes known,
Can truly disembody on its own.

Against property
There is but one thing to be said for Mammon:
If I just had it. But of course I don't.

Contamination of the Species
The human race when by capital ruled,
Is like a rare diamond, smeared with poo.

Tucholsky's Excess[45]
Our dear soldier is not so bad at all.
Not a murderer, just when duty calls.

The Perennial Fruit of Knowledge
From Adam did Beelzebub Heaven earn,
Adam received a banana in return.

Modrow
The man wants Socialism, so he says.
He surely shows it in funny ways.

On the splitting of the left-wing magazine "Slaves" into the left-wing magazines "Slaves" and "Slaves Uprising"
To perish you must your unity disown.
The weak man is the weakest when alone.

45 In 1931, the left-wing writer Kurt Tucholsky wrote in an opinion piece: "Soldiers are murderers". The sentence caused outrage (and remained contentious till the 1990s). It led to an accusation against his publisher at the time. After the war, pacifists in West Germany, who quoted this sentence, were repeatedly brought to court with leading politicians demanding convictions.

Unfortunately so
For civil rights, the bourgeois make a fuss.
Rights of the workers they seldom discuss.

Reminiscence of the Spree
We heard them call: One people and one nation.
So too had bawled the national revolution.

GDR in the concrete
Here you found it irksome, pleasant over there?
A state's a system, twit, in case you weren't aware.

Safety Precautions
Balconies, of course, have railings fit.
You need a wall at the edge of a pit.

Practice of morality
To be good is little, the right deed merits praise.
Put an end to infamy, is what Voltaire says.

Socialism
Shows us through its recent abolition
How indispensable is its mission.

Here's to the 21st Century
Even I was born among blood and shit.
The start is not always the prettiest

Good manners
Go under, man, but take heed while you go.
Don't drift. The future looks to you, you know.

Farewell to the Second Millennium
Those thousand years certainly came up short.
But ahead, comrades, to the third or fourth.

[not later than 1995/96]

The Thirty Tyrants[46]

Some are found in past and present
With an itch to jump the queue.
People weak and self-indulgent,
They were found in Athens too.
Back then there were thirty counted,
Who abroad the flames did stoke
Or at home their woes recounted,
Feeling they were special folk.

As then Sparta Athens' ships had
Sunk and so its victory won,
Inside Athens, we could say that
Misery had just begun.
Ah, the wall, so long and pretty,
Razing it, the victor's ploy,
Which had guarded in the city
Everlasting wealth and joy.

To the thirty aforementioned
Was dispatched the victor's call,
To the emigres despondent,
To the local grumblers all.
And as tyrants, no less grander,
They were hoisted on the throne.
This wrote Sparta's Prince Lysander
And he made it widely known.

And they flocked to all the places
That with wine and women wait,

46 Oligarchy installed by Sparta after it defeated Athens in the Peloponnesian War in 404 BC.

And dictated in all cases
Laws of yore to reinstate,
And they stole with grasping fingers
Cattle, fodder, houses, land,
And an army of whip-slingers
Taught us ne'er to take a stand.

Who had for the costs donated
Of the wars on Sparta's plate,
Empire in the east located,
'Twas the mighty Persian state.
Now with five years barely passing
Persia did not feel the same.
Sparta's growth, its troops amassing,
Persia had to change the game.

And so Persia gold invested,
Athens got a long new wall
That around the city rested
And its enemies could stall.
And the tyrants one by one
Into exile did return,
Silently, with glory none,
Or to grumbling, as we learn.

Thirty villains and their thunder,
Do we hear of them today?
History put them with their plunder
In a footnote tucked away.
Or still less. Maybe it's simply
Nothing but a silly song,
Just a snatch that passes limply
To be lost in worldly throng.

[not later than 1998]

My Precious Nation

Just as no wraith nor spirit can surpass
The unicorn in beauty and in wisdom,
Just as the diamond trumps all crystal glass,
And caviar all culinary stardom,
Just as the panther tops all forest beasts,
And Greta Garbo other whores unseats,

So once did stand apart my precious nation
From all the empires of the world that rose,
This country where nobody starved nor froze.
For each there was a roof, an occupation.
How can I praise a vision so immense?
This much I say, it made total sense.

One's wish to blossom forth was not in vain.
The souls took shape, flesh and bones did too.
All higher posts the poorest could obtain.
What's fair for men, was fair for women too.
From neither superstition, nor from debt
Would its proud heart submit to any threat.

No sickness too, for which there was a cure,
Would go neglected by the doctor's art.
No burden either, this you can be sure,
Could set the pauper and the prince apart.
No plutocrat could issue us commands,
Alone to profit from our toiling hands.

Oh how enlightened, and so full of cheer,
With freshness full, with new ideas blooming.
Life today, yet tomorrow was so near,

This was the mission of the nation's planning.
To speak of it a joy, when all's said and done,
A state it was, which all crime did shun.

Who could outshine the pyramids? Indeed,
Could the Kremlin, Sansscouci, Versailles?
No fort, cathedral, castle could succeed
Our dear wall was the apple of my eye.
With gates secure and sturdy towers above.
Truth be told, with it I fell in love.

In days of youth, this was not my station,
It was not in this land that I was born.
But I took freely to my breast this nation,
In it to breathe until the grave I'd sworn.
The concord with the grave came to no good,
But fortune shone on my days of manhood.

This dog world lets us, it is no mirage,
Forgo ideas, but not espionage.
Who's to blame? Let me state it clear,
The KGB. It was nigh twenty year
With Harvard or with Langley[47] in cahoots
On how to overthrow us by the roots.

The Soviet power, it did give us life.
And in our backs did also stick the knife.
Have no illusions though, we're of one heart,
Not even betrayal can tear us both apart.
Enough, for now, of such vague criteria
For Prussia's troubled future with Siberia.

47 Langley refers to the CIA. The CIA headquarters are located there.

Strange is the sun, which was once so dear.
And once so lush the lands beneath this sky
As shadows creep before my clouded eye.
From time to time, I must hold back a tear.
One weeps for Hellas, but 'tis seldom said,
For a state institution tears were shed.

Let me reflect on those who were its founders,
With wit and will, they did it bestow,
To reach for goals most human and not flounder.
So few remain. Let me say this, though,
From one so old to one so near the end.
For Alfred Neumann were these verses penned.

[not later than 1998]

1990

Now already it's three weeks of mine
In the final epoch of decline.

Holding forth in parliament, a pastor.
Leipzig puts its faith in a conductor.[48]

Wrecked and ruined all the factories.
And the proletariat agrees.

Just West Kashubian faces all around.[49]
And Botho Strauss can as a poet count.

My girlfriend too appears quite reticent.
Food and income worries leave her spent.

So she can but partially agree
To enjoy the evening in my company.

As for me, no weakness, not a jot,
I'm not anyone, she too is not,

And so follow what I do to her,
Heights, then we almost without a stir

And with quiet calm, Glenfiddich drinking,
See behind the roofs the epoch sinking.

48 In October 1989, the conductor Kurt Masur mediated between civil rights activists and the SED leadership in Leipzig.

49 West-Kashubian faces – an allusion to the West by way of an allusion to the West German writer Günter Grass, who often pointed out that his mother was a Kashubian, a member of a small ethnic group living in Poland.

[not later than 1998]

Fragile Multi-People State

Fragile multi-people state,
Oh Germany, how will it end?
Two worlds in neither word nor gait
Each other comprehend.

In union forced, together pressed
By Russia's bear was done.
The nation East, the nation West,
As if they were but one.

The nation East, the nation West,
One kingdom is too small.
One common language they possess,
No common thoughts at all.

There is no patch, no stitch, no glue
To mend so deep a cleft.
To live as one no good would do,
Just bile and spleen are left.

So Germany, just set them free
Your gloomy sons and daughters.
From Rhine to Isar, 'tis my plea,
Out of your narrow borders.

Oh let them breathe, let them flee,
We wish they may obtain,
That when they're out of sight, maybe
We like them once again.

Autonomy was on the bill,
To win it was no game.
Two whole countries better still,
Than one gone up in flames.

[not later than 1998]

Venus and Stalin

She, bathing her feet, doth wear no such robe,
To keep from the water she'd need to take care.
In summer so serene all eyes free to probe,
Her world famous chest and her bare derrière.

He, lies outstretched, at the edge of the brook
With the aid of a typist, goes over his notes.
Lest anemoi blow the leaves of his book
Away. Pebbles to this task he devotes.

He is prone to let his paternal eyes
On Venus' smouldering loins come to rest,
While she, quite immersed in her enterprise,
Does raise with both arms a leg to her breast.

The irresistible glow of this duet,
Such splendour that seems to go on forever.
True love and the power of the Soviet
Can be but imagined when together.

[not later than 1999]

Monument to a Monument (2)

What's this red rock in the local sand,
Blocks and slabs cast asunder?
This granite strewn about the local land.
Brought by an ice age, I wonder.

They're Lenin's remains and only last year
His image they did destroy and bury.
When they toppled Stalin, then it was clear,
Lenin would be gone in a hurry.

Lenin's image the terror can deride,
Though his words cannot be untaught.
His statues the terror can surely capsize,
Though not his thought.

The Party

Once two million, now barely
A handful can we avail.
The reason they're weak? Clearly
Gorbachev's betrayal.

With no courage in their breast.
Their spirit, it is shaken.
Who in them did once invest,
Sorely was mistaken.

Ach folks you rotten rabble,
He who trusts you, errs.
Today you want apples.
Tomorrow it's pears.

But when things take a turn,
Both things and your luck,
From the grave you'll return
With the giggles struck.

Now skipping and jumping
With your little minions
Spring of your offspring
Party of four millions.

[not later than 1999]

Now-time

Since that turnaround so dire
Sombre is the poet's view,
All his hopes are dashed entire
In the circumstances new.
Still he stands anticipating
Something that's illuminating.
Then he thinks: Why should I care?
Where there's nothing, nothing's there.

Though indifferent to partaking
In all courteous exchange,
He must kill the hours of waking,
So he feigns there's nothing strange.
Files his nails each week, he does it
Not with zest, but force of habit,
Sometimes kisses Chloë's breast,
Force of habit, not with zest.

Over coffee, idling listless,
News of capital he reads,
Negro states that it suppresses,
Killing, raping, where it leads,
Young and aged, men and women,
Then he notes with satisfaction
That the scribe at any rate
Can't compose a sentence straight.

At the apex of finances,
Nonconforming to its way,
He approaches nature's sources
With a wish to holiday.

Loving summer, winter hating,
Nothing that is worth debating.
Duty calls, a verse to pen
So he does it now and then.

A Playlet

The Bishop of China

Persons
The Emperor KANG XI
His 4th son YONG ZHENG
The SIGNOR DE TOURNON, Patriarch of Antioch
MAIGROT, the Bishop of China
PARENNIN, a Jesuit
Time: 1705. Place: Peking.

The Emperor Kang Xi, when giving audience, sits, his feet on a foot cushion, at a table flanked by two fans shaped like a peacock butterfly made of peacock feathers on long poles. Behind him he has a screen with a canopy of dragon heads. The screen is decorated with a group of four characters. The characters mean: Worship the Lord of Heaven. His son Yong Zheng has his place within a corresponding, but smaller arrangement. When the curtain rises, both of them are stretching their legs. Kang Xi, Yong Zheng.

KANG XI I think, Fourth one, that I do not wish to continue the audience now. There are actually minutes in which one likes to be emperor. The meeting with the man just now made me happy, an expression I rarely use. I don't want anything to ruin my mood again.

YONG ZHENG My Imperial Father, it's nothing more than just one delegation that's still waiting.

KANG XI I recommend you never force yourself to do Emperor's work. Emperor's work must not be done listlessly. No, I've decided we're breaking up.

Tournon, Maigrot, in their ecclesiastical attire. They enter and throw themselves flat on the ground.

KANG XI Who let these characters in? I don't insist that governing should be a pleasure. But if for once it is. . . What am I saying? Take the letter of audience from them, the old bloke has it in his hand.

YONG ZHENG *does so* Let go. Don't squirm.

KANG XI Read aloud.

YONG ZHENG From the Secretary of the Council Chamber for Customs and Ceremonies.

KANG XI Who else? What does the note say?

YONG ZHENG *reads* "His Eminence Thomas Maillard de Tournon, Patriarch of Antioch, who feels compelled to inform His Imperial Majesty of the unfortunately unfavourable judgment of the Holy See concerning the case brought against him. Accompanied by His Eminence Maigrot, Bishop of China."

KANG XI Bishop of China, eh?

YONG ZHENG What species are these?

KANG XI Christians I think. Send them away.

YONG ZHENG Why?

KANG XI Can't you see they're carrion flies?

YONG ZHENG You know I'm here to learn.

KANG XI So learn, pest. But we'll make it short, if you don't mind. *He and Yong Zheng take their places. Kang Xi* All rise. *All stand up. Kang Xi to Tournon* You are the Patriarch of Antioch?

TOURNON Yes, most humbly in waiting, it is I.

KANG XI Very nice. Tell me, how is the weather in your Antioch?

TOURNON I cannot say, august ruler. I haven't ever been there.

KANG XI Oh, but you definitely should.

TOURNON I would like to, but they have a Sultan there who for the time being prevents me from heeding your advice.

KANG XI The man just argues and argues.

TOURNON Antioch is part of Syria, you must know.

KANG XI I don't have to.

TOURNON It is in the hands of heathens.

KANG XI What are heathens?

TOURNON Damned souls. Non-Christians.

KANG XI *to Yong Zheng* Is that lesson enough for you?

TOURNON Signor Maigrot is the Bishop of China.

KANG XI Where is he based?

TOURNON In the diocese of Conon.

KANG XI Where?

TOURNON In Fukian province.

KANG XI Fukian, at least that's located in the world.

TOURNON Yes, it is just across from Formosa.

KANG XI I am well aware that Fukian is just across from Formosa.

TOURNON It is this longish large island.

KANG XI I know what Formosa is, I've just conquered it – but what do you say he's the bishop of?

TOURNON Of China.

MAIGROT I am the spiritual head of the Chinese.

KANG XI So I heard right, I wanted to make sure. Allow me to introduce my fourth son to the gentlemen. Yong Zheng is here because I'm instructing him in the conduct of imperial affairs.

TOURNON If he is bothersome, I'll certainly point it out to you.

YONG ZHENG I thank the gentlemen for their patience in enduring the presence of one who is unworthy.

MAIGROT *pats Yong Zheng on the head.* Well, my little baldhead.

YONG ZHENG Take your hands off, you long-nosed motherfucker.

TOURNON I beg forgiveness for my spiritual brother's mistake. It was unintentional.

KANG XI Yong Zheng, it's better for the likes of us if you stay a little agreeable. It's far too easy for us to be rude, hence it's beneath our dignity. Do you understand?

YONG ZHENG Yes. A rude emperor would be like an elephant with the cast of mind of a fighting cock.

KANG XI The fourth one, you see, he understands quickly. My son and I express our gratitude to you, Signor de Tournon, for having travelled so far to do us the honour of your visit. *Dismisses them with a wave of the hand.*

YONG ZHENG What could the stinker have meant?

KANG XI With what?

YONG ZHENG That he's supposedly the bishop of China?

KANG XI The words an emperor has to ignore in his life, if gathered in a chorus, would drown out the voice of the sea. – The gentlemen are no longer needed. *Waits for them to go.* The audience is ended. *Waits for them to go.* Go now. Out. Do you want to beat it, or would you rather that I get you slow-sliced?

TOURNON Slow-sliced, what does the exalted ruler mean?

MAIGROT They scrape the flesh from a living body. They use tongs, scissors, knives and planes, also some kind of awl. They have artists who know the course of every vein and feed on every nerve wherever it reaches, being careful not to injure the more important ones. There is a competition among the executioners: who can slice the longest. Unfortunate victims scream for months without being granted death.

TOURNON But that's diabolic.

KANG XI Haven't I heard it said that you burn your wrongdoers alive, preferably on a low fire?

TOURNON Don't you do that?

KANG XI Never.

MAIGROT The wood here is too expensive for them. They can't afford a decent auto-da-fé.

KANG XI The punishment of slow-slicing is not at all made use of in the Middle Kingdom.

MAIGROT I know better than that.

KANG XI It is only envisaged for cases of parricide and insulting the emperor.

MAIGROT As I said.

KANG XI No Chinese murders his father. No Chinese insults his Emperor.

MAIGROT Three of my lambs, I was a witness, were slow-sliced for peeing on an ink painting of Emperor Tai Tsung.

KANG XI That is something else. They weren't Chinese, they were Christians.

TOURNON We don't want to pre-empt the topic. I wish to raise a complaint, august ruler, of disrespectful conduct towards

His Holiness the Pope whom we serve. A man of loathsome appearance was admitted to audience before us though we were already waiting.

KANG XI Where did you gather that from?

TOURNON He passed us in the antechamber as he left you.

KANG XI That man was a farmer.

TOURNON You talk to a farmer while keeping the servants of His Holiness waiting?

KANG XI I have promoted him to Mandarin of grade eight rank.

TOURNON Straight from the field?

KANG XI On the contrary, on condition that he stays in his field. He now has four embroidered ducks on his breastplate. His name will be written in golden letters on the wall of a small pagoda.

TOURNON You are doubtless proud of this?

KANG XI A little.

TOURNON The Church too blesses the poor.

KANG XI I didn't bless him, I promoted him to a high civil servant, and not because he was poor, but for his services to the agriculture of his province. What impression did he convey when he passed you?

TOURNON Exhausted.

KANG XI Exhausted, was that your impression?

TOURNON Yes.

KANG XI It might well be true. As I said, I wish the gentlemen a safe journey home.

TOURNON We thank you. But doesn't your Imperial Majesty desire to know in a nutshell the outcome of the case that Your Imperial Majesty has just lost?

KANG XI I can't have lost a case because it's not possible to bring any such case against me.

TOURNON The case against Imperial Majesty was filed in 1645.

KANG XI 1645, when would that be?

YONG ZHENG It has to do with the birth of one of their gods. Father Parennin constantly tries to teach me the conversion, but it constantly gets too complicated for me.

MAIGROT The case began in the second year of the 21st Dynasty, the illustrious Manchu dynasty.

KANG XI The year after my father Schun Chi took office?

MAIGROT The same.

KANG XI That's sixty years ago.

MAIGROT Your Majesty may discern from this the care that has been taken in Your Majesty's case.

KANG XI Someone has been carrying on a case against me for sixty years without my coming to know even a syllable of it?

TOURNON That you may come to know of it immediately is the purpose of my visit.

KANG XI Signor de Tournon, I give you permission to present your report.

TOURNON Your Majesty is very gracious.

KANG XI Before you begin, Signor de Tournon.

TOURNON Yes?

KANG XI The occupation of an emperor is the most difficult of all occupations. It's exactly a million times as hard to think about a hundred million people as it is to think about a hundred. Predecessors of mine became quite cranky as a result. One whose profession is China does not know any individual Chinese. It bespeaks far greater benevolence to give a province an incorruptible governor than to annul a foot-lashing decreed for a dozen innocents. In consideration of this point, I would like to request you to spare me any inconsequential matters.

TOURNON There is no such danger. I will only touch on matters of the first order.

KANG XI Much that is important to ordinary people is not important to an emperor. I wanted to bring this to your attention. I feel something like pain at the mention of trifles. I entreat you not to let yourself go. Let us make a pact, Signor de Tournon: I will allow you to speak freely and you will spare me trifles.

TOURNON Very well. In the year . . . At the stated time, His Holiness the Pope received . . .

KANG XI Who?

YONG ZHENG The Pope is the head priest of all Christians.

TOURNON No, of all human beings. He lives in Rome.

KANG XI Where is this?

YONG ZHENG Rome is situated on a promontory in a small inland sea in the West.

KANG XI These unbelievers are unbearable.

TOURNON You know the countries of the West?

KANG XI To the west are India and Russia, with whom we have trade dealings and foster satisfactory relations.

TOURNON But beyond that, still further west?

KANG XI Yes, an indefinite number of additional tribes are said to dwell there, I am well aware of that, and I find it distasteful to speak of it. All this digresses into the indeterminate.

TOURNON Do you know these tribes?

KANG XI Only the most important.

TOURNON The most important are enough.

KANG XI The Netherlands and Portugal.

TOURNON How so these in particular?

KANG XI I seized Formosa from the Netherlanders.

TOURNON Yes, and the Portuguese seized Macao from you.

KANG XI No impertinence.

TOURNON Aren't I right?

KANG XI Just because you're right doesn't entitle you to be impertinent.

TOURNON The most important country in the West is Italy.

YONG ZHENG France, Germany, Sweden.

TOURNON All these exist, my prince, but Rome is the capital.

KANG XI I have heard of Rome, of course.

TOURNON It would be difficult to imagine otherwise.

KANG XI Is Herr Caesar still alive?

TOURNON He was murdered long ago.

KANG XI Would you convey my condolences to his widows?

TOURNON You seem to have very old news at your disposal.

KANG XI We also have the latest. Mr. Marco Polo paid us a visit not long ago and told us about everything.

TOURNON Marco Polo? But that was three hundred years ago.

KANG XI Not so long ago, like I said.

TOURNON May I continue?

KANG XI Certainly.

TOURNON In that said year, with which I had the honour to begin, a plea reached the Pope both from the Dominican brothers and from the Franciscan brothers against the sacrilege of idolatry committed in the Chinese Empire with the complicity of the Jesuits. The Pope handed the matter over to the Inquisition that very same week.

KANG XI Ahem?

TOURNON To the Ministry for Open Questions of Faith, it conducts investigations. The investigation revealed. Firstly. On a certain day of the year, called Confucius Day, the Chinese worship those of their idols they call ancestors in the form of prayer, burning of incense, and slaughtering of sacrificial animals; but they especially pay homage to the creator of this custom, a certain Confucius.

KANG XI We do this; for we are a pious people.

MAIGROT You are my pious witch, said Satan to the magician's wife.

TOURNON Leave it be, Bishop.

MAIGROT I can hardly leave bad alone as good.

TOURNON For the moment. Secondly. The Chinese who believe in idols on such a scale do not believe in God.

KANG XI Not in God?

TOURNON Instead of God, they believe in heaven.

KANG XI This is quibbling. It's the same.

TOURNON Heaven is a haze, a direction, a principle, whatever. Heaven is material, but God is immaterial. Heaven cannot be God.

KANG XI Nobody said that. I'll prove it to you. You can find the proof here, here over my imperial head, in these characters. *Points to the characters behind him.* It says here: Worship God who is in heaven.

MAIGROT That's not what's there.

KANG XI It's right here. There, here it is.

MAIGROT It's not there.

KANG XI Why don't you just read. The sign for "worship". The sign for "God". The sign for "being present, being". The sign for "heaven".

MAIGROT That's not how I read it.

KANG XI Fine, but I'll explain it to you.

MAIGROT I say it's not there. I not only speak Chinese, I also read and write it. What's there is something else.

KANG XI Then what?

MAIGROT Whatever you want, just not that.

TOURNON Keep quiet for once. – Both deadly sins came to pass with the approval and abetment of the Jesuits. In this section of the investigation, an interim interdict was issued against the above heresies.

KANG XI Interim?

TOURNON Until the final decision by the Pope. The Jesuits insist that, based on a deeper understanding, Chinese and Christians have the same faith.

KANG XI Right. That's an interpretation with which they feel comfortable.

TOURNON Yes, the Jesuit fathers did a brilliant job of defending you. In 1656, twelve years after that year in which the case began, the Ministry for Open Questions of Faith permitted you to practice your customs, provided that no superstition is implied.

KANG XI Your open ministry of faith permits me to practice my customs?

TOURNON That's how free of prejudice we are.

KANG XI It is I who allow you your customs. I granted legal sanction thirteen years ago to spreading the principles of the Christians in China.

TOURNON Not of the Christians. Of the Jesuits.

KANG XI Well, I don't know any other Christians. The Jesuits are great scholars and wise men. They have mastered astronomy, geography and the mathematical arts.

TOURNON May I continue? – A further charge on the same point was brought by Signor Maigrot, Bishop of China. The Chinese are idolaters in regard to Confucius and their ancestors, and they are materialists in regard to the nature of God.

KANG XI It is rather the other way around. God lives in heaven, and the ancestors are dead, they are only commemorated by the state and under the direction of officials.

TOURNON The two theses, the one of His Eminence Maigrot and the one His Majesty just deigned to enunciate, were handed over to the Sorbonne for examination.

KANG XI Eh?

TOURNON The University of Paris. It has the ultimate jurisdiction. The Abbé Boileau represented the position of the Catholic Church against the Jesuit Father le Comte. As you can well imagine, the great city of Paris held its breath. The verdict was handed down. The praise of the Jesuits for the Chinese, that they were simple and uninformed, but otherwise of an exemplary disposition, is to be classified as heretical, blasphemous, godless. This is the verdict of the Sorbonne. This is the verdict of Clemens XI. He commands you to return from your errant ways and let Christianity flourish and spread unhindered in China.

KANG XI Who commands me to do this?

TOURNON Clemens XI.

KANG XI Eh?

TOURNON The Pope.

KANG XI Oh, that one again.

TOURNON Under threat of excommunication. His Holiness sent

me as his legate to Your Majesty in the year 1700.

KANG XI 1700?

TOURNON Five years ago.

KANG XI Why didn't you leave then?

TOURNON I left. My journey took five years.

KANG XI Five?

TOURNON Two of them for me to learn Chinese. Three more were taken up by the local immigration authorities.

KANG XI The immigration authorities?

TOURNON This is what I have to report.

KANG XI Remind me, Yong Zheng, to confer a pennant on my border guards.

TOURNON Today I stand here and declare you an apostate. A heavy penance awaits you and for me there's a cardinal's hat.

KANG XI I am very angry with you, Signor de Tournon.

TOURNON Exalted Ruler, I am only the messenger.

KANG XI Messenger, of what?

TOURNON The judgement you deserve.

KANG XI What, judgement? I had entreated you, Signor de Tournon, not to bother me with trifles.

TOURNON From which trifle do you accuse me of having failed to spare you?

KANG XI These pronouncements of taste from your Inquisition and your Sorbonne and your Signor Pope Clemens, it was all nothing but one damn trifle. Your permission to speak stands revoked. Would you you leave now?

TOURNON My task has been accomplished.

KANG XI Then go.

TOURNON Your Majesty only has to declare that you accept the judgment of the Holy Church.

KANG XI At most, whether I accept the verdict.

TOURNON No, that. You have to.

KANG XI And if not?

TOURNON The interdict.

KANG XI Another trifle.

TOURNON Excommunication, a trifle?

KANG XI Excommunication by your church is all the same to me.

TOURNON Maybe not quite the same. Any honest Christian people who conquer any portion of China would ipso facto be sure of doing a godly deed. The Russians, for example, when they tried to move their border into the Chinese inland. . .

KANG XI It didn't go well for them. Now they pay me tributes.

TOURNON Yes, but when you went to war with them you had a very clear conscience and you hadn't as yet been damned by the Holy Father. The English government. . .

KANG XI You mean the East India Company?

TOURNON You are aware that the English are not content with being restricted to Canton as the only open Chinese port. They demand access to other ports.

KANG XI What do they need ports for? Canton is enough to ship my porcelain to England.

TOURNON It could be that one port is not enough for the goods that the English wish to ship to China.

KANG XI What do we need from England?

TOURNON Opium.

KANG XI And the English might just fall upon the idea of making war on me so that they can sell their opium to China?

TOURNON The excommunication might give them such an idea.

KANG XI The cannons on the English ships won't strike better because they have the Pope's blessing.

TOURNON Much better.

KANG XI Yong Zheng, the man you and I call our favourite teacher, could you ask him to join us when his time permits.

YONG ZHENG I understand. I'll go right away.

KANG XI Please do continue with your threats. Who else do you intend to unleash against us besides the English and the Russians?

TOURNON I do beg Your Majesty to calm down. Much is only half as bad as it sounds. We've done a lot of work with your language, but we often can't bring the subtleties out. You see, the English and the Russians, they aren't even Christians themselves.

KANG XI The English and the Russians, not Christians?

TOURNON Not in the least.

KANG XI I would have bet they are. What is the name of the religion to which the English and the Russians adhere?

TOURNON They don't have the same one.

KANG XI Each a different one?

TOURNON The only thing that unites them is the common effort to misunderstand Jesus Christ.

KANG XI Nothing surprises me anymore.

TOURNON We don't want to give the impression that we have anything else in mind with Your Imperial Majesty than Your Imperial Majesty's best interests.

KANG XI What do you have in mind?

TOURNON Just put your soul in the hands of my spiritual brother. He will lead you safely to God.

KANG XI He of all people?

MAIGROT Yes, you happen to belong to my congregation. Believe me, I myself am ill at ease with the likes of a congregation member like you. I didn't get to choose you.

KANG XI *to himself* I must maintain my composure, they're savages. – What objections do you have to my soul?

MAIGROT Bringing yellow souls to God, that's my task in this country.

KANG XI Evidently.

MAIGROT I too will one day stand before my Maker. Maigrot, my son, says God, why do you bring me souls that are yellow?

KANG XI Indeed, there might be a difficulty in this. *To himself* They're savages, Emperor, you should not hate them. – What does the Patriarch say?

TOURNON Yellow souls, that's a wretched old wives' tale. The bishop is a pious man, he is not a scholar. He does not know that souls cannot possibly be yellow. Souls have no colour.

MAIGROT No colour, are you sure?

TOURNON Quite sure.

MAIGROT But the day the dead rise from the grave?

TOURNON What's with that day?

MAIGROT Well, they will rise from a million graves, along with all their yellow bodies. What a sight for God.

TOURNON God is very well able to wash them if He wishes. Ignore his rambling. He's racking God's brains. What presumption. The greatest of all emperors cannot rack God's brains.

MAIGROT I deserve this rebuke.

TOURNON Only the Pope can rack God's brains.

MAIGROT I see that I have sinned.

TOURNON There is one question, however: When God decided to beget the Saviour with a human virgin, – Your Majesty himself would not want to suppose that he could just as well have considered a flat-chested Chinese woman as Our Blessed Virgin Mary.

Yong Zheng

YONG ZHENG My imperial father, Father Parennin, as commanded. *Exit.*

KANG XI Parennin, come in.

Parennin, Yong Zheng leading him by the hand. Parennin with a full beard and a very tall, brimless hat. His habit is yellow and its cut resembles that of a Chinese robe, and his shoes, with their upward pointed tips, are also Chinese.

KANG XI We are in great need of you. *Parennin starts to fall on his feet. Kang Xi jumps up and stops him.* We don't need that among friends. *Introduces him* Father Parennin, my Minister of Science and my friend. *To Parennin* Have the goodness, Father, to join our conversation. We, the bishop, the patriarch, and I, are struggling with a few contentious issues. My mind is no match for the astuteness of these gentlemen.

MAIGROT Brother Parennin, is that a Christian dress you are

wearing, or a Chinese one?

PARENNIN Even a Christian has a country in which he is at home.

MAIGROT Yes, until the day it gets pulled out from under his ass.

PARENNIN I am humbly aware of this.

MAIGROT *takes Parennin's hat off* The tonsure, at least that's still there.

PARENNIN Shouldn't it be?

MAIGROT There could have been a pigtail hidden under the cap.

TOURNON Brother, what purpose do such accusations serve?

MAIGROT You come from Europe, you haven't suffered for decades at the hands of this person. He can dress up as a Chinese, why can't he have grown a pigtail? *He hops around and squeaks as if it's Parennin he's aping.* Oul Fathel which alt in Heaven . . .

KANG XI I beg you to be seated, Father.

PARENNIN Still the old joker, Maigrot? How are you, Signor de Tournon? *He sits down on a cushion with his legs crossed.*

KANG XI Would you do me the favour of indicating to your fellow ministers the point where the flat earth has its centre?

PARENNIN It's not that easy for me to carry out your command. Please do remember, I am a Christian.

KANG XI He who calculates the floods of the Huang He so well for me and predicts the eclipses of the sun and the moon, how can I blame him, if he also believes a little in Christ. *He comes out from behind his table and places himself in the middle of the stage; he won't sit down again until the end of the play.* Isn't it the case that the centre of the earth is in this building, in the very place that happens to be marked by that inlay on which I happen to be standing? Parennin is a geognost whose knowledge amazes everyone. Tell the gentlemen, where is the centre of the earth?

PARENNIN If you so command.

KANG XI I'm just requesting you

PARENNIN The centre of the earth as you ask me . . .

KANG XI Now without further ado, quickly, amaze me, where is it?

PARENNIN In Rome.

KANG XI Are you deceiving me now, or have you been deceiving me all my life?

PARENNIN I deceived you. I withheld the truth from you, my lord and emperor, you were not yet enlightened enough to bear it. You still had need of this superstition.

KANG XI Let's leave geography aside. It is a matter of two points.

PARENNIN I know the points.

KANG XI It is about the worship of the ancestors.

PARENNIN The ancestors are demons.

KANG XI The ancestors are simply our deceased forefathers.

PARENNIN You pray to them.

KANG XI What could be wrong with that?

PARENNIN Prayers only make sense when they are heard.

KANG XI We hope they are.

PARENNIN Dead people who hear are demons.

KANG XI You never found anything wrong with the custom.

PARENNIN How could I, there were imperial ancestors among those who were worshipped.

KANG XI And Confucius?

PARENNIN Confucius, but he's not a demon. Confucius is the devil.

KANG XI It used to be possible to have sensible conversations with you.

PARENNIN I will have to answer for this before my Maker and above all before my superiors in Rome.

KANG XI Don't make me uncertain about the other point. I will prove to you the correctness of my point of view.

PARENNIN Your god is the sky, a natural phenomenon.

KANG XI Is this group of letters the sign for "Worship the Lord of Heaven"?

PARENNIN Of course it is.

KANG XI And does it not mean: Worship – God – who is – in heaven?

PARENNIN It means: Worship – the heaven – which is – the

godhead.

KANG XI The characters can mean both, my reading as much as yours.

PARENNIN That, you must admit, is your trick.

KANG XI Not a trick, but I confess I don't dislike it. I like terms that mean a lot.

PARENNIN An intentional vagueness. The rabble is to understand that God is in heaven, and the scholars that heaven is God, but that is devotion to drifting dust and empty spaces. It makes physics into religion. To be sure, the Sorbonne, which isn't stupid, managed to figure it out.

KANG XI Why didn't you tell me all this earlier?

PARENNIN You would never have let me into your palace. You have to enter the enemy's house through his door.

KANG XI The enemy's house?

PARENNIN Now I'm leaving it through my own.

KANG XI You're leaving Peking?

PARENNIN My general has declared me a heretic and recalled me.

KANG XI To Rome?

PARENNIN I'm on my way to Korea.

KANG XI Korea? This kingdom is ill-disposed to all strangers and sends them zealously to their deaths.

PARENNIN Yes, that's why we Jesuits go there.

KANG XI Is that what you heretics are good for?

PARENNIN The cross awaits the Christian in every place.

KANG XI You uttered the very same sentence during our first conversation after you arrived here.

PARENNIN It is true.

KANG XI And then you got me to admit the Jesuits, against the opposition of my officials who oversee the rites. And then you let him come. You fought him in Rome, but in China you let him win the day. And then your work here was done, the Bishop of China, the interdict, the East India Company, all your work. And now you go to a new cross that awaits you.

PARENNIN Things can be looked at that way.

KANG XI The Jesuits handle the cross more skilfully than Jesus Christ did.

PARENNIN Being skilful is not a crime.

KANG XI Not for thieves. *To Yong Zheng* You will be the most powerful prince in the world, but you should fear one kind of people, they are priests who wish you well.

YONG ZHENG Put him to death.

KANG XI I can't put a man to death for whom I've done so much. *To Parennin* I shall think of your maps and mathematical proofs from time to time, not without nostalgia. Good luck in Korea.

YONG ZHENG I forbid that. Father, you cannot let him go, out of respect for your ancestors.

KANG XI Don't be rude to your ancestors, Yong Zheng. These people have been carrying on a case against me for sixty years, no-one should rebuke us Chinese in haste. Measures produce counter measures. Better to choose the most modest measure over the most extreme, that is an unshakeable principle of politics.

YONG ZHENG There are cases where the most extreme measure is the most modest of those that promise success.

KANG XI That may be so, but it is not professional. – Signor Maigrot, Signor de Tournon, by law I could kill you both.

MAIGROT You won't impress me with severity. We Catholics are used to severity.

KANG XI He who does not shy away from the highest penalties, that's the sign of the born criminal. Bishop Maigrot must leave China today without delay.

MAIGROT I object.

KANG XI Bishop Maigrot's congregation in Conon will be beheaded.

MAIGROT You'd have to cut off three thousand heads.

KANG XI Three thousand, but the price is worth it. – You were very brave in front of me, Signor de Tournon.

TOURNON No, honestly, I didn't believe till the end that a savage would dare contradict the Holy Father.

KANG XI The Legate de Tournon, Patriarch of Antioch, will be exiled and held in custody in Macau.

TOURNON I thank the august ruler for dismissing me to my Portuguese friends.

KANG XI The governor is Portuguese, and he has gathered not a few rabble against me in that city of mine. But have a care not to forget that Macao remains a part of China. No part of China will ever cease to be a part of China, not until the day time ends. *To Yong Zheng* Escort the gentlemen out into the street. *Exit.*

YONG ZHENG Come along.

TOURNON Prince, you will succeed your father to the dragon throne.

YONG ZHENG Maybe. And?

TOURNON Perhaps a few words of understanding on the way, a small arrangement for later?

YONG ZHENG Since you remind me of later. If any of you ever set foot on Chinese soil again, I'll have him slow-sliced alive, and the same, as surely as I'll be Emperor, goes for every damned Christian under the sun. Come along.

THE END

For the Record

Autobiography

Saint Benedictus, who I'm told was born in the year 480, was primarily concerned with solving the problem of how to live as happily as possible on earth and yet just about make it to heaven. I, who I'm told was born in 1928, am concerned (after changing what has to be changed) with the very same problem.

Persons Index

Achilles. Greek hero of the Trojan War, and the central character of Homer's epic poem *Iliad.*

Andropov, Yuri (1914–1984). Leader of the Soviet Union from 1982 till 1984.

Aristophanes (c. 446–c. 386 BCE). Comic playwright of ancient Greece, sometimes referred to as the Father of Comedy.

Aristotle (384–322 BCE). Greek philosopher and scientist during the classical period in ancient Greece.

Auffenberg, Joseph von (1798–1857). German playwright.

Bahro, Rudolf (1935–1997). East German social scientist; prominent GDR dissident.

Baier, Walter (*1954). Chairman of the Communist Party of Austria from 1994 to 2006.

Baierl, Helmut (1926–2005). German playwright and former vice president of the GDR Academy of Arts.

Bakunin, Mikhail (1814–1876). Russian revolutionary; founder of the anarchist tradition.

Bebel, August (1840–1913). Leading figure of the social democratic movement in Germany, cofounder of the SPD.

Becker, Holger. Former editor of the newspaper "Neues Deutschland", former chief editor of the newspaper "junge Welt".

Belicke, Sibylle. Wife of Hacks' friend Kurt Belicke (1929–1993, East German writer).

Berg, Jochen (1948–2009). German writer, editor of the literary magazine "Sklaven".

Bernstein, Eduard (1850–1932). German political theorist and leader of the SPD.

Beuchel, Fred. Co-founder of the Communist Platform, an association within the German Left Party.

Beuys, Joseph (1921–1986). West German artist and art theorist.

Bierce, Ambrose (1842–c. 1914). American short story writer and poet.

Biermann, Wolf (*1936). Songwriter, poet, and former East German dissident.

Birch-Pfeiffer, Charlotte (1800–1868). German playwright and actress.

Blair, Tony (*1953). Leader of the Labour Party and Prime Minister of the UK from 1997 to 2007, who supported the US-led wars on Iraq (1998 and 2003), the NATO bombing of Yugoslavia (1999), and the US war in Afghanistan (2001).

Blanqui, Louis Auguste (1805–1881). French socialist who believed that revolution should be carried out by a small group of professional revolutionaries.

Böll, Heinrich (1917–1985). West German writer; winner of the 1972 Nobel Prize for Literature.

Brandt, Willy (1913–1992). Leader of the SPD and chancellor of the FRG from 1969 to 1974; known for his policy of Ostpolitik, i.e. détente with Soviet-bloc countries.

Branstner, Gerhard (1927–2008). East German writer, known for his writings on humour and as an author of Science Fiction.

Brecht, Bertolt (1898–1956). German playwright and poet; forced to flee Nazi Germany in 1933, returned from exile in 1948 to East Berlin where he set up his own theatre, the Berliner Ensemble.

Brezhnev, Leonid (1907–1982). Leader of the Soviet Union from 1964 to 1982. In the 1970s he tried to normalize relations with the West and to promote détente with the US.

Brie, André (*1950). German politician representing the SED, then the PDS, now Die Linke.

Bukharin, Nikolai (1888–1938). Russian Soviet economist and political figure.

Bush, George W. (*1946). US President from 2001 to 2009; ordered the 2003 war on Iraq.

Castro, Fidel (1926–2016). Leader of the Cuban revolution and head of state of Cuba from 1959 to 2008.

Charles IX of France (1550–1574). King of France from 1560 till 1574; the astrologer Nostradamus was counselor at his court.

Charles of England (1600–1649). King of England; executed in 1649.

Churchill, Winston (1874–1965). Prime Minister of the UK from 1940 till 1945 and again from 1951 to 1955.

Clausewitz, Carl von (1780–1831). Prussian general and military theorist; author of *On War*, a work on military strategy.

Confucius (551–479 BCE). Chinese philosopher and reformer; his teachings were highly influential across East Asia.

Corneille, Pierre (1606–1684). French poet and dramatist, considered the creator of French classical tragedy.

D'Alema, Massimo (*1949). Italian left-wing politician; Prime Minister of Italy from 1998 to 2000.

Demetrius (1582–1606). Russian tsar between 1604 and 1605; the first of three pretenders to the Russian throne, all referred to as False Dmitry.

Dewey, John (1859–1952). American philosopher.

Diogenes (412/404–323 BCE). Greek philosopher who lived in a wine barrel.

Duchamp, Marcel (1887–1968). French painter and sculptor.

Dühring, Eugen (1833–1921). German philosopher, whose ideas about socialism prompted Friedrich Engels to write his rebuttal, *Anti-Dühring*.

Duke Carl August of Weimar (1757–1828). Grand Duke who invited Goethe to the court of Weimar.

Dumas, Alexandre, père (1802–1870). popular French writer, author of such novels as *The Count of Monte Cristo* and *The Three Musketeers*.

Dutschke, Rudi (1940–1979). West German sociologist, prominent representative of the leftwing student movement of the 1960s.

Engels, Friedrich (1820–1895). German philosopher and political theorist; co-founder with Karl Marx of Marxism.

Faber, Joachim (Baby) (1913–1986). Composer who lived in Munich.

Fischer, Joschka (*1948). Former prominent member Germany's Green Party; foreign minister of Germany from 1998 to 2005.

Fülberth, Georg (*1939). West German political scientist, member of the DKP. Having studied German Literature, Fülberth also made a name for himself in the 1990s by propagating and disseminating Hacks' work.

Garbo, Greta (1905–1990). Swedish American actress; one of the most glamorous and popular Hollywood film stars.

Glucksman, André (1937–2015). French philosopher: began as a Maoist, turned into a human rights activist after disillusionment with communism.

Goethe, Johann Wolfgang (1749–1832). German writer; prominent representative of German classicism.

Gorbachev, Mikhail (1931–1922). General Secretary of the CPSU (1985–1991), leader of the Soviet Union at the time of the collapse of socialism; introduced policies of glasnost and perestroika.

Gossweiler, Kurt (1917–2017). German Marxist historian; leading historian of the GDR.

Gramsci, Antonio (1891–1937). Italian Marxist philosopher and political theorist; founding member of the Italian Communist Party (PCI); arrested by the fascist government in 1926 and kept in prison until his death in 1937.

Grass, Günter (1927–2015). West German writer, author of "The Tin Drum".

Gregorek, Karin (1941–2023). German actress and theatre director.

Gremliza, Hermann L. (1940–2019). German journalist; founder and editor of the left-wing journal "*konkret*".

Gysi, Gregor (*1948). Leader of the PDS, forerunner of The Left (Die Linke).

Hagen, Eva Maria (1934–2022). German actress and singer.

Hammarskjöld, Dag (1905–1961). Swedish economist; Secretary-General of the United Nations from 1953 till 1961.

Havel, Václav (1936– 2011). President of the Czech Republic from 1993 till 2003.

Hegel, G.W.F. (1770–1831). German philosopher; one of the founding figures of modern Western philosophy.

Heine, Heinrich (1797–1856). German writer, regarded as one of Germany's greatest lyric poets.

Hertzfeld, Lothar. Co-founder of the Communist Platform, an association within the German Left Party.

Hesiod (c. 700 BCE). Ancient Greek poet.

Hilferding, Rudolf (1877–1941). Austrian-born Marxist economist and theorist of the SPD during the Weimar Republic; author of *Finance Capital* (1910).

Hitler, Adolf (1889–1945). Leader of the Nazi Party since 1921 and of Nazi Germany (1933–45).

Hobsbawm, Eric (1917–2012). British Marxist historian.

Hobson, John A. (1858–1940). English economist; best known for his book *Imperialism. A Study.*

Holbein, Franz Ignaz von (1779–1855). Austrian playwright and theatre director.

Holz, Hans Heinz (1927–2011). West German Marxist philosopher.

Honecker, Erich (1912–1994). leader of the GDR from 1971 until its collapse in 1989.

Houwald, Ernst von (1778–1845). German playwright.

Hue, Robert (*1946). General Secretary (1994–2001) and President (2001–2002) of the Communist Party of France.

Huxley, Aldous (1894–1963). English novelist; author of *Brave New World.*

Iffland, August Wilhelm (1759–1814). German playwright.

Jabal. Biblical figure in the Old Testament, brother of Jubal.

Jacob, Bruno and Emmi. Veterans of the KPD and then of the SED.

Johnson, Lyndon (1908–1973). US President from 1963 to 1969; authorised the vast escalation of the Vietnam War.

Jubal. Biblical figure in the Old Testament, seen by some as the 'inventor of music'; brother of Jabal.

Kabila, Laurent (1939–2001). Congolese revolutionary, ally of Lumumba; after Lumumba's murder, he led revolt against Mobutu and was joined by Che Guevara; President of Congo 1997–2001.

Kang Xi (1654–1722). Emperor (1661–1722) of the Qing (Manchu) dynasty (1644–1911/12) in China.

Kautsky, Karl (1854–1938). German Marxist theorist and leader of the SPD.

Kemal, Mustafa (Atatürk) (1881–1938). Turkish nationalist leader and founder of the republic of Turkey.

Kerensky, Aleksandr (1881–1970). Russian revolutionary; leader of Provisional Government from July to November 1917.

Khrushchev, Nikita (1894–1971). General Secretary of the CPSU (1953–1964) and leader of the Soviet Union (1958–64), known for his policy of "de-Stalinization" and "peaceful coexistence" with the capitalist West.

Kipphardt, Heinar (1922–1982). German writer.

Kohl, Helmut (1930–2017). Chancellor of the FRG from 1982 to 1998; presided over the incorporation of the GDR into the FRG in 1990.

Kotzebue, August von (1761–1819). German playwright.

Kropotkin, Peter (1842–1921). Russian revolutionary; theorist of anarchism.

Krüger, Marian. Co-founder of the Communist Platform, an association within the German Left Party.

Krüss, James (1926–1997). German author of children's and picture books.

Küchenmeister, Claus (1930–2014). German writer; member of the Writers' Association of the GDR.

Kurz, Robert (1943–2012). German Marxist philosopher.

Lassalle, Ferdinand (1825–1864). One of the founders of the social democratic movement in Germany.

Lenin, Vladimir (1870–1924). leader of the Russian Revolution, Marxist theorist and founding head of the Soviet Union till his death in 1924.

Leonardo da Vinci (1452–1519). Italian painter, sculptor, architect, and engineer of the Renaissance period.

Lessing, Gotthold Ephraim (1729–1781). German writer of the Enlightenment.

Longo, Luigi (1900–1980). General Secretary of the Communist Party of Italy (PCI) from 1964 to 1972.

Lopushansky, Konstantin (*1947). Russian film director and writer.

Louis XVI (1754–1793). King of France; executed by guillotine during the French Revolution.

Lumumba, Patrice (1925–1961). African anti-colonial leader, first Prime Minister of Congo after independence from Belgium. His toppling and assassination were sponsored by the US and Belgium with support from the then UN Secretary-General Dag Hammarskjöld.

Luxemburg, Rosa (1871–1919). Polish-born German revolutionary and Marxist theorist, co-founder of the KPD.

Lysander (died 395 BCE). Spartan leader who destroyed the Athenian fleet in 405 BCE.

Mahdi, Muhammad al (1844–1885). Sudanese cleric who led the Mahdist Revolt against British-ruled Egypt.

Maigrot, Charles (1652–1730). French Catholic priest; in charge of the missions of China.

Mann, Thomas (1875–1955). German writer; winner of the 1929 Nobel Prize for Literature.

Mao Tse-tung (1893–1976). leader of the Chinese Revolution and founder of the People's Republic of China, which he led from 1949 until his death in 1976.

Marcuse, Herbert (1898–1979). German-American philosopher, prominent member of the Frankfurt School of critical theory.

Marx, Karl (1818–1883). German philosopher and political theorist; co-founder with Friedrich Engels of Marxism.

McCarthy, Joseph (1908–1957). US Senator, who during 1950–1954 led the hunt for Communists in the government and public life, which became known as the McCarthy Era.

Michelangelo (1475–1564). Italian sculptor, painter, architect, and poet of the Renaissance period.

Mistral, Frédéric (1830–1914). French writer; winner of the 1904 Nobel Prize for Literature.

Mobutu, Joseph Désiré (1930–1997). Congolese politician; deposed the democratically elected government of Patrice Lumumba with the support of Belgium and the US.

Modrow, Hans (1928–1923). Last chairman of the Council of Ministers of the GDR; regarded as a Gorbachevist reformer in the last years of the GDR.

Mozart, Wolfgang Amadeus (1756–1791). Austrian composer of the classical period.

Mpolo, Maurice (1928–1961). Congolese political figure and ally of Patrice Lumumba; murdered along with Lumumba in 1961.

Müller, André (1925–2021). West German writer; friend and collaborator of Hacks.

Müller, Heiner (1929–1995). East German playwright and poet.

Müllner, Adolf (1774–1829). German playwright.

Mussolini, Benito (1883–1945). Founder of the National Fascist Party and leader of Fascist Italy (1922–43).

Myron (c. 480–440 BCE). Sculptor of the classical period in ancient Greece.

Napoleon Bonaparte (1769–1821). Also known as Napoleon I; French general and Emperor of France (1804–1814/15); introduced the Napoleonic code, the first modern civil code and the prototype of later civil codes.

Napoleon III (1808–1873). Nephew of Napoleon I.

Nasser, Gamal Abdel (1918–1970). President of Egypt from 1954 till his death; leader of the Arab world, co-founder of the Non-Aligned Movement in 1961.

Nechayev, Sergey (1847–1882). Russian revolutionary associated with the Nihilist movement.

Nenni, Pietro (1891–1980). Leader of the Italian Socialist Party (PSI).

Nero (37–68 CE). Roman emperor: known for the apocryphal story that he fiddled while Rome burned in a great fire.

Neumann, Alfred (1909–2001). Member of the GDR Council of Ministers from 1962 till 1989; close associate of Walter Ulbricht.

Newton, Isaac (1642–1727). English physicist and mathematician, prominent figure of the Scientific Revolution of the 17th century.

Nostradamus (1503–1566). French astrologer who wrote cryptic prophesies about future events.

Odysseus. Legendary Greek king; key figure in Homer's epic poems the *Odyssey* and the *Iliad.*

Okito, Joseph (1910–1961). Congolese political figure and ally of Patrice Lumumba; murdered along with Lumumba in 1961.

Orwell, George (1903–1950). English novelist; author of *Animal Farm.*

Osama bin Laden (1957–2011). Co-founder of al-Qaeda, military commander of the Mujahideen in the Soviet-Afghan War, mastermind behind the 9/11 attack on the New York World Trade Center.

Parennin, Dominique (1665–1741). French Jesuit missionary to China.

Perón, Juan (1895–1974). President of Argentina (1946–52, 1952–55, 1973–74) and founder of the Peronist movement.

Petrak, Heinz (1929–2014). Marxist scholar of the GDR.

Perugino, Pietro (c. 1446/1452–1523). Italian Renaissance painter; Raphael was his most famous pupil.

Plato (428/427–348/347 BCE). Philosopher of the classical period in ancient Greece.

Pyrgoteles (4th Century BCE). Celebrated gem-engraver of ancient Greece.

Raphael (1483–1520). Italian painter and architect of the Renaissance period.

Raupach, Ernst (1784–1852). German playwright.

Reimann, Max (1898–1977). Chairman of the West German KPD.

Reinhold, Otto (1925–2016). Marxist economist of the GDR.

Rothschild, Lionel (1808–1879). British banker, member of the prominent Rothschild banking family of England.

Saint Benedictus (480 –548). Italian Christian monk, writer, and theologian.

Saint Boniface (c. 675–754). English missionary and leading figure in the Christianisation of Germany.

Schiller, Friedrich (1759–1805). German dramatist and poet; prominent representative of German classicism.

Schlegel, Friedrich (1772–1829). German philosopher, writer, literary and art critic, historian and classical philologist; leading representative of Romanticism.

Schmidt, Arno (1914–1979). German writer.

Schröder, Gerhard (*1944). SPD leader and Chancellor of the FRG from 1998

to 2005.
Scribe, Eugène (1791–1861). French dramatist and librettist.
Shakespeare, William (1564–1616). English playwright and poet; widely regarded as the greatest English writer.
Shaw, George Bernard (1856–1950). Irish playwright; winner of the 1925 Nobel Prize for Literature.
Smith, Adam (1723–1790). Scottish economist and social philosopher of the Enlightenment; author of *The Wealth of Nations.*
Sohn, Manfred (* 1955). German politician representing the DKP, then the Left Party, now returned to the DKP.
Solzhenitsyn, Aleksandr (1918–2008). Prominent Soviet dissident.
Sophocles (c. 497/6–406/5 BCE). One of the three Greek tragedians of Athens during the classical period of ancient Greece.
St. Borromeo (1538–1584). Archbishop and cardinal of the Catholic Church.
Stalin, Joseph (1878–1953). Georgian-born Soviet revolutionary who led the Soviet Union from 1924 to 1953 during the period of industrialisation, collectivisation of agriculture and the defeat of Nazi Germany.
Stehr, Heinz (*1946). leader of the DKP; its chairman from 1990 to 2010.
Steiniger, Klaus (1932–2016). German journalist and book author in the GDR.
Stirner, Max (1806–1856). German philosopher.
Stoph, Willi (1914–1999). Chairman of the Council of Ministers of the GDR from 1964 to 1973, and from 1976 until 1989.
Strahl, Rudi (1931–2001). East German playwright, novelist and poet; one of the most popular playwrights of the GDR.
Strauss, Botho (*1944). West German writer.
Subcomandante Marcos (* 1957). Leader of the Zapatista National Liberation Army and of the Chiapas uprising in Mexico.
Swift, Jonathan (1667–1745). Anglo-Irish writer; author of *Gulliver's Travels.*
Synge, J.M. (1871–1909). Irish playwright, author of the comedy "The Playboy of the Western World".
Thurber, James (1894–1961). American writer and cartoonist.
Tito, Josip Broz (1892–1980). Communist leader and President of Yugoslavia till his death; co-founder of the Non-Aligned Movement.
Tolstoy, Countess Sofia. Leo Tolstoy's wife and author of *The Diaries of Sofia Tolstoy.*
Tolstoy, Leo (1828–1910). Russian novelist of realistic fiction; author of *War and Peace* and *Anna Karenina.*
Tournon, Charles Thomas Maillard de (1668–1710). Papal legate sent to the Chinese court to settle the rites controversy – whether Chinese ceremonies honouring Confucius and family ancestors were incompatible with Christian belief.
Trotsky, Leon (1879–1940). Russian Marxist revolutionary and political theorist; leader of anti-Stalin opposition.
Tübke, Werner (1929–2004). East German painter.
Tucholsky, Kurt (1890–1935). German satirical poet, essayist, social critic.
Ulbricht, Walter (1893–1973). German revolutionary; leader of the SED and the

GDR from its founding till 1971.
Varga, Eugen (1879–1964). Hungarian-born Soviet economist.
Vellay, Rolf (1927–2001). German communist and journalist in the FRG.
Villon, François (c. 1431–after 1463). Best known French poet of the Late Middle Ages.
Voltaire (1694–1778). French writer, historian, and philosopher and defining figure of the Enlightenment.
Wagenknecht, Sahra (*1969). Prominent member of the PDS, then of the Left Party.
Wagner, Richard (1813–1883). German composer of music dramas.
Warhol, Andy (1928–1987). American artist and leading representative of the pop art movement.
Weber, Elle (*1930). Founding member of the DKP.
Webster, John (c.1580–c.1632). English dramatist; contemporary of Shakespeare.
Wiede, Anna Elisabeth (1928–2009). German playwright and author of children's books; wife of Peter Hacks with whom she moved from Munich to East Berlin in 1955.
Wilson, Robert (*1941). American playwright and director.
Wolf, Markus (1923–2006). Prominent member of the GDR intelligence service (commonly known as the Stasi); head of the foreign intelligence department.
Woytila, Karol Józef (1920–2005). Pope John Paul II from 1978 till 2005; credited with being instrumental in the downfall of socialism in Europe.
Yong Zheng (1678–1735). Emperor (1722–1735) of the Qing (Manchu) dynasty (1644–1911/12) in China.
Zhdanov, Andrei (1896–1948). Soviet official and cultural ideologist.

Translators and Sources

SOURCES

AM1	André Müller sen.: Gott hält viel aus. Zweihundert Anekdoten über Peter Hacks. Eulenspiegel Verlag, Berlin 2009
AM2	Aus dem Nachlass, Briefwechsel mit André Müller, Anlage zum Brief von Hacks an Müller vom 23.2.1990
DjH	Der junge Hacks, 5 vols., hg. v. Gunther Nickel. In Zusammenarbeit mit Meike Bohn. Eulenspiegel Verlag, Berlin 2013
HW	Peter Hacks: Werke, 15 vols., Eulenspiegel Verlag, Berlin 2003
LBG	Peter Hacks: Lieder – Briefe – Gedichte. Verlag Neues Leben, Berlin 1974
MH	Peter Hacks: Marxistische Hinsichten. Politische Schriften 1955–2003, hg. v. Heinz Hamm. Eulenspiegel Verlag, Berlin 2018
UP	Unpublished
WDH	Peter Hacks: Was ist das hier? 130 Anekdoten über Peter Hacks und dreizehn anderweitige. Eulenspiegel Verlag, Berlin 2003

TRANSLATORS

SM/KK	Shaswati Mazumdar and Kai Köhler (Editors of this volume)
MD	Michael Dorrity
FDK	Franziska and Dmytri Kleiner

The translations by MD and FDK are from: *On Imperialism, Socialism, and the Responsibility of the Artist*. Translation by Michael Dorrity. Perspektive Internationale, Berlin 2020. These translations were edited by SM/KK for this volume. All other translations are by SM/KK.

TITLE | TRANSLATORS | SOURCE

(Auto-)biographical

Personal Particulars (not later than 1990) | MD | AM2

Anecdotes (by Hacks) (around 2000)

Maxim | SM/KK | WDH

A Beginning | SM/KK | WDH

A Small Request | SM/KK | WDH

An Uncommon Expression | SM/KK | WDH

The Eleventh Thesis on Director's Theatre | SM/KK | WDH

Materialism | SM/KK | WDH

Déjà vu | SM/KK | WDH

Hacks' Limitation | SM/KK | WDH

The Pointlessness of Catastrophes | SM/KK | WDH

In Defence of the Measures | SM/KK | WDH
Cowardice and Drama | SM/KK | WDH
Moment of Contemplation | SM/KK | WDH
Prerequisite for an Award | SM/KK | WDH
Landscapes without frills | SM/KK | WDH
Nicolaiviertel, Berlin | SM/KK | WDH
Gorbachev | SM/KK | WDH
Presumptuous Freedom Fighters | SM/KK | WDH
Fraudulent Labelling | SM/KK | WDH
Urban Planning | SM/KK | WDH
Optimism Debate | SM/KK | WDH
Anecdotes (by André Müller in collaboration with Hacks) (around 2000)
In Defence of Brecht | SM/KK | AM1
Harmful Poems | SM/KK | AM1
Custom | SM/KK | AM1
New Idea | SM/KK | AM1
Dangerous Times | SM/KK | AM1
Assessment | SM/KK | AM1
Lofty Pique | SM/KK | AM1
A Small Error | SM/KK | AM1
TV Delights | SM/KK | AM1
Last Flash | SM/KK | AM1
Strictly Conservative | SM/KK | AM1
Frustration | SM/KK | AM1
Conclusion | SM/KK | AM1
Humble Question | SM/KK | AM1
Loyalty to Oneself | SM/KK | AM1
Envy | SM/KK | AM1
Historical Lessons | SM/KK | AM1
Final Word | SM/KK | AM1

Political
Letter to the German-African Society (1962) | SM/KK | UP
On the War of Aggression in Vietnam (1965) | MD | MH
A Revolution Against the State (1968) | MD | MH
How Are Things in Socialism's Public Offices? (1976) | MD | HW 15
The Latest from Biermann (1976) | MD | HW 13
The Little Men With Their Ballheads (1988) | MD | MH
Letter to a Lady in Paris (1989) | MD | MH
The Worst Socialism Is Still Better Than the Best Capitalism (1992) | MD | MH
The Task Before Us: The Restoration of a Revolution Cut Short (1998) | MD | MH
The Names of the Left (2000) | MD | HW 13
Georg Nostradamus or The Predictions of Professor Fülberth (2000) | MD | HW 13
Dispute at the Wailing Wall (2001) | MD | MH
In the End they Even Understand It (2003) | MD | MH

On Art and Aesthetics
Literature in the Age of Science (1959) | MD | HW 13
Brecht's Aesthetics (1961) | SM/KK | HW 13
Answers to 4 questions (1963) | SM/KK | HW 13
From the Foreword to the essay collection "The Poetic" (1966) | SM/KK | HW 13
The Entrance March of Demetrius, Or: Theatre as Pomp (1966) | SM/KK | HW 13
Art and Revolution (1971) | MD | HW 13
Butzbach Author Survey (1972) | SM/KK | HW 13
Saving Christianity from the Christians (1972) | MD | HW 15, 185–186
From the Literary Legacy: Note on Young Writers in the GDR (mid 1970s) | MD | MH
Information for America (1975) | SM/KK | HW 13
[Ideal and Utopia] (1976) | SM/KK | HW 13
Foreword to "Determinations" (1986) | SM/KK | HW 14
From the essay collection "Poetic Commerce" (1987)
Ancient Trade
The Mule | SM/KK | HW 14
On Certain Errors in Marx and Engels
The Artworks of the Porter | MD | HW 14
Under the Media, the Muses fall silent (1990) | SM/KK | HW 13
Left-Wing Art (2001) | MD | MH

Stories and Poems
[Two Heavenly Tales] (not later than 1947) | SM/KK | DjH 4
Ameli and the Frog King (1953) | SM/KK | DjH 4
The Man from Sing-Sing (1953) | SM/KK | DjH 4
The Wench Factory of Tahoua (1954) | SM/KK | DjH 4
The Royal Court Moves House (Children's Fantastic Tale) (1998) | SM/KK | HW 11
Children's Poems
Frau Thousand-feet Must Wash Today (1952) | SM/KK | HW 10
Errors (1949/1964) | SM/KK | HW 10
Ladislaus and Komkarlinchen (1964) | SM/KK | HW 10
News of the Life of the Peramblers (1964) | SM/KK | HW 10
October Song (not later than 1957) | MD | LBG
Strike Song (1958) | SM/KK | LBG
Lumumba's Death (1962) | FDK | HW 1
You Shall Deny Me Nothing (not later than 1971) | SM/KK | HW 1
1. 8. 1973 (1973) | MD | HW 1
Ask Not Whether Love is Worth It (not later than 1974) | SM/KK | HW 1
Asides (between 1974 and 1988)
The Party | MD | HW 1
Whimsical | MD | HW 1
Democratic Press | MD | HW 1
CIA | MD | HW 1

Trying Times (1988) | SM/KK | HW 1
The Little Unicorns (1988) | SM/KK | HW 1
Make Haste, O You Hours (1988) | SM/KK | HW 1
Couplets (after 1989)
Shaw | MD | HW 1
Imperialism, a Vampire | MD | HW 1
Wonder of the Battle in Congo | MD | HW 1
Monster of the Century | MD | HW 1
FRG | MD | HW 1
Surveillance State | MD | HW 1
Organised Crime | SM/KK | HW 1
Voting Day | MD | HW 1
Crash | SM/KK | HW 1
Against Property | SM/KK | HW 1
Contamination of the Species | MD | HW 1
Tucholsky's Excess | MD | HW 1
The Perennial Fruit of Knowledge | MD | HW 1
Modrow | MD | HW 1
On the Splitting of the Left-Wing Magazine "Slaves" into the Left-Wing Magazines "Slaves" and "Slaves Uprising" | MD | HW 1
Unfortunately So | MD | HW 1
Reminiscence of the Spree | SM/KK | HW 1
GDR in the Concrete | MD | HW 1
Safety Precautions | MD | HW 1
Practice of Morality | SM/KK | HW 1
Socialism | MD | HW 1
Here's to the 21st Century | MD | HW 1
Good Manners | SM/KK | HW 1
Farewell to the Second Millennium | MD | HW 1
The Thirty Tyrants (1995/96) | SM/KK | HW 1
My Precious Nation (not later than 1998) | MD | HW 1
1990 (not later than 1998) | SM/KK | HW 1
Fragile Multi-People State (not later than 1998) | MD | HW 1
Venus and Stalin (not later than 1998) | MD | HW 1
Monument to a Monument (not later than 1999) | MD | HW 1
The Party (not later than 1999) | MD | HW 1
Now-time (not later than 1999) | SM/KK | HW 1

Playlet
The Bishop of China (1999) | SM/KK | HW 8

For the Record
Autobiography (1965) | SM/KK | HW 13